ULTIMATE SHOPPER™

A local's handbook to
O'ahu's most unique shopping

(100% made in Hawaii)

COPYRIGHT © 1998 BY THE BESS PRESS, INC. & FXPRODUCTIONS

All Rights Reserved

Printed in Hawaii By Valenti Brothers

ISBN: 1-57306-081-X

THE
BESS
PRESS

Published by The Bess Press 3565 Harding Avenue, Honolulu, HI 96816

Foreword

A word about this book...

Every year when the wedding anniversary comes up, I begin to sweat—preparing myself for the inevitable "That's nice, honey" and a return trip to the store for an exchange. Let's face it, I need guidance when it comes to shopping. I need a book like this one—and I'm sure many others are in the same boat.

But this book wasn't created just for the shopping impaired. It's for anyone who shops—period. It was designed to make shopping a fun, exciting, and successful activity for all shoppers and reflect the true—the Ultimate—Hawaii shopping experience, one shaped by Hawaii's diverse ethnic mix of peoples and cultures and found only in Hawaii—an eclectic array of merchandise (and the people behind it) tailored to meet the needs of residents and the expectations of visitors.

Ultimate Shopper™'s Oʻahu Edition is a celebration of 100 stores that epitomize the flavors of Hawaii—new stores, local favorites, out-of-the-way finds, and traditional family businesses. More important, it introduces the reader to the people behind these unique businesses—the "hearts and souls" of the shops. Among those you'll meet in this book are the founders, owners, merchandise buyers, store clerks, husbands, wives, children, and your neighbors.

In compiling this distinctive mix of stores, we were constantly surprised and inspired by the stories behind the businesses. Tales of labors through adversity before finally "getting it right"; of dynamic inspiration through an accidental event; of family obligation to carry on a tradition that turned into a private passion. But what came through in virtually all cases was a resolve to constantly improve themselves, and a belief in the purpose and place their businesses have in the hearts of Hawaii.

We asked the owner(s) of each store to write, in their own words, about what makes their business a unique one. Space doesn't allow for more than a taste of the "whole story"; so if what you see intrigues you, drop by and speak with the owners. We found them all to be down-to-earth people, more than willing to "talk story."

While you're sure to find a few "old friends" in the pages of this book, we know that you'll be pleasantly surprised by the number of new ones you'll discover. Before compiling a list of possible candidates for inclusion, we spoke with retailing experts, marketing directors, store owners, and some of the most inveterate shoppers in the state. We made every effort to find the most unique, whether in product offering, history, location, services, or just plain "feel." You may not agree with our choices, or we may have inadvertently left off a great local "find." If so, we'd love to hear your thoughts. Please write, call, fax or email us at FX with your suggestions. We'll be constantly updating the book in an effort to offer the best possible selections.

We at Ultimate Shopper™ believe strongly in supporting and nurturing those things that make Hawaii unique. Everyone who helped create this book lives here and shares the same interest in preserving paradise as you do. We are locals in the best sense of "Aloha," because we believe that to be "local" is a "state of heart," not limited by race or how long one has been in Hawaii. We love our home, and I believe it shows in our dedication and spirit.

The remarkable businesses featured here also reflect what's best about our beloved Hawaii. The owners are experts and innovators in their respective fields who offer more than simply a product for sale. What you acquire from them is not only a unique product of quality, but personal attention—local-style; a sense of place; and a host of other intangibles.

So use this book to become the "Ultimate Shopper." Have fun! Share it with friends and family, give it to a visitor... In the process, you're sure to find "that perfect something," explore a new part of the island, learn a little more about Hawaii, and make new friends.

Hugh O'Reilly (FX)

Contents

NOHEA GALLERY

ISLAND ART & FINE CRAFTS

L M

Nohea Gallery celebrates the work of over 450 painters, printmakers, woodworkers, ceramists, glass artists and jewelers. More than 85% of these artists live and work in the Islands. Customers who visit craft fairs and studio sales are pleasantly surprised to learn that our prices are comparable. If you visit us often you're sure to meet many of the artists—many weekends we offer demonstrations and lessons too. Additional locations at the Kahala Mandarin Hotel (737-8688) & Sheraton Moana Surfrider (923-6644). Web: www. nohea gallery.com.

We believe art is for everyone!

Gail & Laurie (mother & daughter) opened Nohea Gallery in 1990. Gail's mother was a painter in the islands since the 50's, nurturing a love of island art in her family. "The artists we work with are committed to giving the customer real quality and fair prices. That commitment to excellence across the price spectrum has earned Nohea a place in the lives of our customers. We feel very grateful to be a part of this community and we welcome you to it!"

Mon.- Sat.   10.00a - 9.00p
Sunday   10.00a - 5.00p

Ward Warehouse
Honolulu, HI 96814
☎ 596-0074

Map4 / D5 (W1) **1**

EKI CYCLERY

BICYCLES & ACCESSORIES

At Eki Cyclery service and commitment span three generations. With a history like that, it's no wonder people from around the islands seek out this store to satisfy their cycling needs. A wide selection of top-quality brands like Trek, Schwinn, and Nishiki/Raleigh fill our spacious showroom. Whether you're a kid or a senior, looking for a cruiser or full suspension, collectibles or comfort, we can help you get your wheels turning.

Serving Hawaii's families since 1911

Jay and Jayne Kim (owners)
When this family business needed steering, this husband and wife team took hold of the handlebars. "We make a great team—Jay's zest and knowledge of bikes shines through, while Jayne's pragmatic style keeps us on course."

Mon.- Sat.   9.00a - 6.00p
Sunday   10.00a - 4.00p
1603 Dillingham Blvd.
Honolulu, HI 96817
☎ 847-2005

ANNE NAMBA DESIGNS

WOMEN'S FASHION DESIGN & SALES

Anne Namba Designs was born with the opening of her retail store in 1989. Anne uses the ageless beauty of Japanese kimonos and obis to create unique contemporary clothing for women. Anne's clients include First Lady Hillary Rodham Clinton; the Queen of Soul, Aretha Franklin; Mrs. Sadaharu Oh, wife of Japan's most famous baseball star; and socialite Ann Getty.

Unique designs, beautiful fabrics, flattering lines, and a comfortable fit

Anne Namba (designer)
Anne developed her love for travel and unique clothing while living in Bangkok and Tehran as a child. Educated at the prestigious Fashion Institute of Technology in New York, Anne spent six years as part of New York's fashion industry including the costume department at Radio City Music Hall. Anne's designs have been featured nationally on Lifetime television, and are carried in the Saks Fifth Avenue Folio Catalog, Nordstrom, and Bergdorf-Goodman in New York.

Mon.- Sat. 10.00a - 5.30p

2964 East Manoa Road
Honolulu, HI 96822
☎ 988-9361 Fax 988-4894
annenambadesigns@prodigy.net

Map2 / A3 3

IT'S CHILI IN HAWAII

UNIQUE GOURMET CHILI GIFT STORE

Ever had one of those days when you needed a little extra spice in your life and no matter what you did, you just couldn't get it hot enough? Relax—somebody understands. There's an exciting place where you can fulfill your hottest desires. Chili desires, that is. We're talking about your Hot & Spicy Headquarters in the Pacific: It's Chili In Hawaii, literally, the hottest store around. Our oasis for chiliheads will tantalize your taste buds with made-in-Hawaii and other chili-based products from around the world. If you enjoy cooking with bottled, dried, powdered, or jellied chilis—have we got the HOTS for you! Not quite sure how to use these products? Ken or Gary, both Chili Aficionados, will be more than happy to point you in the right direction with tips on chili preparation, mouth-watering chili recipes, and chili trivia.

The chili capital of the Pacific

Gary & Ken (owners)
Our house of heat hosts an open house every Saturday that's chilihead nirvana. Fresh flour and corn tortillas made in front of you! Samples of chili stews, tamales and other incredible creations guaranteed to arouse those long dormant endorphins. Come join the fun!

Monday 10.00a - 5.00p
Tue.- Sat. 10.00a - 6.00p

2080 South King Street
Honolulu, HI 96826
☎ 945-7070

GLOBAL VILLAGE MARKET

HEMP • AROMATHERAPY • JEWELRY • APPAREL • GIFTS

Global Village Market has gathered an "earth friendly" mix of clothing, jewelry, beads, and gifts from artisans around the world. Explore the assortment of candleholders, vases, and picture frames crafted from recycled glass and aluminum. Sample the fragrance of candles, glycerin soaps, lotions, and essential oils. Feel the hemp, organic cotton, linen, rayon, and natural-blend fabrics that combine in comfortable, casual clothing. Personalize your fashion with straw hats, raffia bags, and jewelry in sterling silver, semi-precious gemstones, dichroic glass, and brass. Or create one-of-a-kind earrings, necklaces, bracelets, and anklets from a vast selection of beads.

Keeping the earth in mind...

Debbie, Dawn & Sharrie Ah Chick (owners)
Family owned and operated, Global Village Market brings together a few of the simple and natural pleasures the world has to offer.

Mon.- Fri.   9.00a - 6.00p
Saturday   10.00a - 5.00p
Sunday   11.00a - 3.00p

306 Kuulei Road
Kailua, HI 96734
☎ 262-8183

Map3 / C2 5

LANCE FAIRLY GALLERY

FINE ART & GIFTS

"You have beautiful things!" is a remark we hear frequently from customers. Besides Lance's magnificent fine paintings of classic Hawaiian scenes, you will also find unique handmade painted gift items displaying the craftsmanship of talented artists: batik clothing and sarongs, decorative glass plates, pillowcases, chimes and mobiles, and jewelry, in vivid colors that remind you of brilliant tropical Hawaii.

An enjoyable & memorable shopping experience for every customer!

The Fairly family
The gallery, in a historic building that survived the 1946 tsunami, is located across from the Sacred Falls State Park— a favorite island hiking spot.

Mon.- Sun. 9.30a - 6.30p

53-839 Kamehameha Hwy
Hauula, HI 96717
☎ 293-9009

HANA PA'A HAWAII

FISHING SUPPLIES

Hana Pa'a Hawaii is your "One-Stop, Full-Service" Fishing Store. Whether you're interested in trolling, shorecasting, spearfishing, or netting, you will find everything you need right here. Novices, commercial fishermen, and everyone in-between can feel confident in the products and services we provide. We offer expert rod and reel repair, line spooling, custom rod wrapping, custom spearguns and shafts, custom netting, and even fresh bait. Our friendly sales staff are all avid fishermen and are always eager to help beginners. They can offer expert advice, rig your lures, or even tie your hooks if necessary. Sometimes they even offer to take you fishing. Come to Hana Pa'a Hawaii for all your fishing needs, or just stop by to swap fishing stories.

Hawaii's most complete fishing store!

Mon.- Fri.	8.00a - 6.00p
Saturday	8.00a - 4.30p
Sunday	8.00a - 12.00p

611-D Middle Street
Honolulu, HI 96819
☎ 845-1865

Sterling, Leopoldo & Rodney

Map4 / C1   7

KAIMUKI HEALTH MARKET

HEALTHY FOODS & SUPPLEMENTS

We opened Kaimuki Health Market in '97 hoping to improve the health of our community's young, middle-aged, and old. Our friendly atmosphere welcomes newcomers as well as those already knowledgeable about a healthier lifestyle. We stock the essentials of a traditional health food store, along with a wide selection of the latest top-quality-brand products: personal care items, books, vitamins and supplements, groceries, herbs, and quick, healthy snacks.

*If you're healthier...
you're happier*

❂
Mon.- Sat. 9.00a - 8.00p

3566 Harding Ave.
Honolulu, HI 96916
☎ 739-2990

Debbie & Daryl Yamaguchi
We're a brother and sister team who always knew we would end up working together. Our quest to live healthier lives led us to the right business opportunity. We found that many of our family and friends were looking for the same thing. The result: Kaimuki Health Market.

SnapShot

PHOTOGRAPHY EQUIPMENT & SERVICES

They said, "The economy sucks!" They told us to downsize like everyone else. But we're just BULLDOG STUBBORN. So instead, we expanded—5 times larger. Now we have created Hawaii's first One-Stop-Everything-Shop. Everything? Well almost! And if we don't have it, we'll tell you why, where, when, or how to get it. But chances are, if it has to do with photography—amateur or professional—we have it, or can get it, or do it. So don't let our ferocious-looking mascot scare you, 'cause deep down, we're just BULLDOG LOVABLE.

Bulldog lovable!

Leroy (mascot)

Mon.- Fri.   8.00a - 6.00p
Sat.- Sun.   9.00a - 3.00p

629 Pohukaina Street
Honolulu, HI 96813
☎ 536-3683

Map4 / D4 9

HAWAIIAN RENT ALL

"GENERAL STORE" OF RENTALS

Why buy an expensive piece of equipment that you will use once or twice in a lifetime when you can rent it for a fraction of the cost? Hawaii Rent-All carries thousands of items that will help you get the job done faster and safer than trying to "make do" or borrow equipment. Our 30+ years of experience enables us to provide exactly the items you need for a wide variety of endeavors, from barbecueing to pipe threading. We have it all!

We rent 'most everything!

Mon.- Sat.   8.00a - 5.00p
Sunday   9.00a - 2.00p

1946 South Beretania
Honolulu, Hi 96826
☎ 949-3961 Fax 955-3959
louihome@aol.com

ARTLINES

A Grand Bazaar

Leave your passport at home and explore an amazing collection of gifts, from Afghanistan to Zaire. Bronze sculptures, wood carvings, crystal balls, mineral specimens, incense, tribal masks, textiles and stained glass blend traditional Folk Art with U.S. contemporary crafts. Images of past civilizations, ceremonial objects, mythological figures and religious artifacts provide a fascinating multicultural backdrop for the unique jewelry collection.

**Cultural
discovery
& ethnic
appreciation**

Saulo & Taso (owners)
The two international artist/owners travel the globe, carefully selecting and importing whimsical gifts and jewelry for every budget. They design and create original pieces featuring quartz, amber, and a plethora of beautiful semiprecious and antique trading beads.

Mon.- Sat.   9.30a - 9.00p
Sunday   10.00a - 7.00p

Ala Moana Center #1226
Honolulu, HI 96814
☎ 941-1445

Map4 / D6 (AM) **11**

THE COMPLEAT KITCHEN

HAWAII'S KITCHEN SPECIALTY SHOP

Since 1976 The Compleat Kitchen has been serving Hawaii's cooks and charming Hawaii's visitors at its Kahala Mall shop in the heart of residential Honolulu. High-quality kitchenware for the serious gourmet sits alongside innovative, one-of-a-kind items for kitchen and home. Our island heritage is reflected throughout the shop in an assortment of tropical-designed textiles and gourmet foods found only in Hawaii. The Compleat Kitchen creates a blend of comfort, uniqueness, quality, and expertise that attracts customers from all over the world.

Cooking is fun-damental!

Mon.- Sat.   10.00a - 9.00p
Sunday   10.00a - 5.00p

Kahala Mall
Honolulu, HI 96816
☎ 737-5827

Marc Villanueva (manager)
"We love to cook and it shows! From classic kitchen gadgets to unique and tasty gifts, you'll discover a world of treasures when you enter our shop."

BRIDAL EMPORIUM

BRIDAL GOWNS AND ACCESSORIES

Nothing is more beautiful than a wedding in Hawaii, but even if you are getting married someplace else, at Bridal Emporium you'll find the finest and most complete selection of gowns for the bride. We also have unique dresses for the bridesmaids, flowergirls, and the mothers of the bride and bridegroom, as well as veils, all other accessories, and much more.

*Our number one priority
is our brides-to-be*

Bridal Emporium staff:
Owners Deanna Overbey and Leslie Nakagawa are Hawaii's foremost bridal salon entrepreneurs. They and their staff have over 30 years combined experience creating beautiful brides and perfect weddings. Visit their modern showroom to find everything you need for the wedding you've always dreamed of.

Mon.- Fri. 10.00a - 7.00p
Saturday 9.00a - 5.00p
Sunday 10.00a - 4.00p

250 Ward Avenue, #170
Honolulu, HI 96814
☎ 596-8281 Fax 593-0032

Map4 / D5 **13**

VINTAGE WINE CELLAR

FINE WINES, SPIRITS & ACCESSORIES

The award-winning Vintage Wine Cellar is the only store in Hawaii that sells wines and spirits from all over the world. Our people visit the owners and winemakers, taste wine, discover new wines, and procure the best (by "best," we don't necessarily mean the most expensive. We mean high quality relative to price). We take pride in our knowledgeable staff who can assist you in selecting the perfect wine for any occasion—from a special bottle for a romantic evening to cases of wine for your big celebration. The cellar receives wine deliveries weekly, so you'll find something new on each visit. Every weekend we host a free in-store tasting, where customers can sample wines from the store's vast selection.

🌐
Mon.- Sun. 10.00a - 7.00p

1249 Wilder Avenue
Honolulu, HI 96822
☎ 523-WINE (9463)

*If you love wines,
Vintage Wine Cellar
is your paradise*

Jay Kam (co-owner)
Allen and Cora Kam turned their
interest in wines into a business.
Now, thirty years later, a member of
a new generation, Jay Kam, has
joined them. All are bona fide wine
lovers.

OCEANIA

ISLAND-STYLE CLOTHING & GOODS

Oceania offers comfortable, fun island styles for everyone from teenager to tutu. Make sure you check out our collection of handcarved wood(!) tropical flowers. Always in bloom—no watering necessary! Two convenient locations are easy to get to from anywhere on Oahu: Aloha Tower Marketplace in town, or on the North Shore at 66-208 Kamehameha Highway. Please call us at 637-4581 for North Shore store hours.

Just the right thing

Barbara Williams (owner)
Barbara loves to be in the stores, helping people to find just the right item.

Mon.- Sat. 9.00a - 9.00p
Sunday   9.00a - 9.00p

Aloha Tower Marketplace
Honolulu, HI 96813
☎ 524-0237

Map4 / D4 (AT) **15**

THE BEAD GALLERY

BEADS, JEWELRY & WORKSHOPS

Tucked away in a quiet, second-floor room near Ala Moana Shopping Center, Honolulu's premier bead store is spacious and comfortable. Clear glass dishes are filled with opalescent, transparent, and faceted beads, in colors ranging from lemon yellow and rose pink to sea green and sky blue. We offer over 10 different monthly workshops, and our friendly beaders at the counter are ready and willing to assist the "bead-ginner." Drop by and string a necklace, create a gift, or begin a hobby that will last a lifetime.

A bead lover's heaven

Jamie & Jason
The store is run by a family of beaders whose skills include seed bead work, metalworking, wire-bending, fiber-weaving, macrame, knotting, fimo beadmaking, lampwork glass beadmaking, and more.

Open 7 days A Week
Call For Seasonal Hours

1347 Kapiolani Blvd #200
Honolulu, HI 96814
☎ 944-2600
email: beadgirl@aloha.net

808 SKATE

SKATEBOARDS & ACCESSORIES

When 808 Skate opened its doors in 1995, it defined skateboarding as a separate subculture. Prior to that, skaters had to be content with just a small section in surf shops. 808 Skate stocks only skateboarding goods, with Hawaii's largest selection of skateboards and skatewear, including clothing, shoes, and accessories. 808's convenient Kailua location—away from town's congestion and high prices—allows it to offer lower prices and... friendly neighborhood service.

Suzan Shinzato Kanzic & Chuck Mitsui (co-owners)
A skateboarder since the age of 10, Chuck opened a skate shop when he became frustrated by the fact that Oahu had no "skate only" shop. Suzan brings her strong business and organizational skills to the company. As a team they are dedicated to bringing the total skate experience to their customers.

Hawaii's only 100% skateboard shop

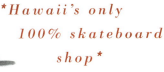

Tue.- Fri.   12.00p - 7.00p
Saturday   10.00a - 7.00p
Sunday   10.00a - 5.00p

26 Hoolai, Suite 800
Kailua, HI 96734
☎ 263-0808

Map3 / C2 **17**

GARAKUTA-DO

JAPANESE ANTIQUES

Garakuta-Do specializes in Japanese antiques and mingei (folk art). Our 7,000-sq. ft. store features displays of a wide variety of antique chests for clothing (Isho dansu), comforters (Futon dansu), business documents (Chobu dansu), kitchen (Mizuya) and even step chests (Kaidan Dansu) which were actually used in old country homes. We also have sea chests (Funa dansu), trunks (Nagamochi), wheeled chests (Kuruma dansu), kotatsu stands (Kotatsu Yagura), money boxes (Zeni bako), sewing boxes (Hari bako) as well as netsuke, hibachi, pot hooks (Jizai kage), clocks, lamps, bamboo flower baskets, dolls, china, bronzes, and a wide assortment of old textiles including kimono and obi.

G H

Japan's past to enjoy now and cherish in the future

Tue.- Sat.   10.00a - 6.00p
Sunday   10.00a - 4.00p

580 North Nimitz Hwy
Honolulu, HI 96817
☎ 524-7755

Wataru Harada (owner) and his wife, Yasuko, established Garakuta-Do in 1983, with a small shop in Waikiki. Buying from auctions held in Japan exclusively for antique dealers, they import six shipments annually. Having operated a small contracting firm in Tokyo doing interior renovation work, Mr. Harada is able to work closely with decorators as well as with connoisseurs of fine Japanese antiques.

OFF THE BOTTOM

HANDMADE LEATHER FOOTWEAR & ACCESSORIES

Off the Bottom offers an affordable and truly original range of footwear. Styles from the simple "Kama'aina" Slipper to the all-terrain, amphibious Holo Sandal, to the lightweight, indestructible Hana Boot are made with top-quality full-grain leather uppers and insoles, EVA memory midsoles, and full-lug rubber soles. Our styles are form-fitting and foot friendly, handcrafted to provide natural, flexible support. Our seams are glued and stitched to ensure long life as well as maximum strength. We also carry a wide variety of leather wallets, purses, belts, bags, handmade jewelry, and accessories.

* Finest quality, ultra-durable footwear for anyone & everywhere *

Gordon Saker (owner/designer)
Gordon began shoemaking to provide people with more durable and comfortable shoes than the ones that were available. Originally from South Africa, he has been in Hawaii since 1992.

Mon.- Sun. 11.00a - 6.00p

66-082 Kam Hwy
Haleiwa, HI 96712
☎ 637-2764

Map1 / B2 **19**

TAPESTRIES BY HAUOLI

UNIQUE APPAREL & ACCESSORIES FOR WOMEN

Tapestries by Hauoli is a unique women's boutique specializing in natural-fiber clothing. Tapestries is known for its large selection of washable linen fashions, including its own line of linens in colorful, creative, and comfortable styles. Lorraine Doo Wong and sister Anita Young shop the global markets for interesting and unusual clothing and accessories that enable women to create exciting wardrobes that express their own personal style. Conveniently located at Ala Moana Shopping Center, Downtown Fort Street Mall and Pearlridge Shopping Center.

Interweaving color, comfort, & creativity

Mon.- Sat. 10.00a - 9.00p
Sunday   10.00a - 6.00p

Pearlridge Center Uptown
Upper Level
☎ 483-0810

Tapestries by Hauoli is one of Honolulu's oldest kamaaina retailers, dating back to 1886, when Lorraine Doo Wong's grandfather founded Yat Loy ("welcome") Company. In keeping with that retail tradition, president Lorraine hopes to pass on the family business to the next generation, son Robbie (11) and daughter Tanya (8), pictured here.

BLACK PEARL GALLERY

JEWELRY AS RARE & EXOTIC AS YOU ARE

Only the highest quality black pearls, set in 18k and 14k designs by award-winning and internationally acclaimed jewelry designers, are what you'll find at Black Pearl Gallery. Since 1983, Black Pearl Gallery has offered original designer creations at its Ward Centre and Aloha Tower Marketplace galleries and at seven locations nationally.

* Sharing aloha with the world through the Tahitian Black Pearl*

The Black Pearl Gallery Crew
Company founder Don Kelly and his wife Mary hand select every black pearl personally to bring you the highest quality. Their long-term relationships with pearl farms in Tahiti enable them to offer you the most colorful, iridescent, and magical pearls. We proudly present designer Travis Duggan, two-time winner of Hawaii's "Designer of the Year" award.

Mon.- Sat.   10.00a - 9.00p
Sunday   10.00a - 5.00p

Ward Centre
Aloha Tower Marketplace
☎ 597-1477 / 524-5552

Map4 / D5 (W2) **21**

ISLAND TREASURES

ART GALLERY

Debbie Costello's Island Treasures Art Gallery features the work of 600 of the finest island artists: koa wood, original paintings and prints, stained glass, ceramics, jewelry, basketry, and much more. The gallery, located on the beautiful windward side of Oahu, offers a wide price range to suit everyone's needs. Island Treasures also offers a bridal registry and worldwide shipping and handling.

Largest selection of handmade-in-Hawaii products

L M

Mon.- Sat.   10.00a - 6.00p
Sunday   11.00a - 4.00p

629 Kailua Road #103
Kailua, HI 96834
☎ 261-8131

Debbie Costello (owner)
Debbie, an artist herself, saw a need for a gallery featuring island artwork at a reasonable price in one location. The gallery opened in 1996 with only 25 artists and has since grown to over 600.

BLACK TIE AFFAIR

MEN'S FORMALWEAR

Black Tie Affair is drastically different from the usual tuxedo store. We maintain a level of service and quality of product not normally associated with tuxedo rentals. A men's formalwear service can have a very positive reputation. Men's formalwear is all we do. Specialization yields a better product.

A reputation for the finest service in men's formalwear

Mike Chong (owner) with daughter Lauren Often accused of expecting perfection, I have brought this attitude to the tuxedo business.

Mon.- Fri.   10.00a - 6.00p
Saturday   10.00a - 5.00p
Appointments Suggested

3566 Harding Avenue
Honolulu, HI 96816
☎ 732-9474

Map2 / C3 23

KO'OLAU FARMERS

RETAIL GARDEN SHOP

Windward community landmark Ko'olau
Farmers sells a wide variety of plants,
cut flowers, and other gardening
products. The staffs of the Kaneohe and
Kailua stores offer shoppers the products
they need along with helpful information
on keeping their plants and gardens at
their best. The Kaneohe store, just a few
blocks from the Hawaiian Memorial Park
and State Veterans Cemetery, is a
popular spot for people buying cut tropical flowers before visiting the cemetery.
Customers like the quality of
the flowers so much that
they also send them to
friends and family on
the mainland. Sending
fresh-cut tropical
flowers to the
mainland is
as simple as a
phone call to the
Kaneohe store.

*A genuine care
for our customers*

Mon.- Sat.   8.00a - 5.00p
Sunday   8.00a - 4.00p

45-580 Kam Highway
Kaneohe, HI 96744
☎ 247-3911

Ko'olau Farmers' staff
Since starting as a farmers'
cooperative in 1941, Ko'olau
Farmers has blossomed into
the premier garden shop of
windward Oahu.

SPLASH! HAWAII

RETAIL SWIMWEAR & SPORTSWEAR

The formula is simple: awesome selection, brand name quality, mix 'n match sizes, separates, and friendly honest help. In addition, a great frequent shopper program and fast, free alterations/repairs. All in a fun, relaxed, convenient location. Find your perfect suit surrounded by sun, sand, and sparkling water. Splash! Hawaii for the styles, smiles, and service you deserve.

Mon.- Sat. 9.00a - 9.00p
Sunday 10.00a - 7.00p

Ala Moana Center
Street Level Makai
Honolulu, HI 96814
☎ 942-1010

Hawaii's
swimwear
leader

Dennis Fallas & Gary McCarty
Friends since they met at Kailua High School on Oahu, Dennis and Gary have worked side by side ever since, first managing other clothing stores and then in 1980 starting their own company. Now, after almost two decades, Splash! Hawaii is an international success and perhaps the most unique and exciting swimwear specialty store in Hawaii.

Map4 / D6 (AM) 5

BOUTIQUE COMME CI COMME CA

ECLECTIC CONSIGNMENT BOUTIQUE

A delightful and affordable collection of gently worn, recycled apparel and accessories for every taste. The Boutique offers a constantly-changing "dream closet" to women searching for that something special unavailable everywhere else.

Classic, eclectic-- Comme Ci Comme Ca

GH

🌐 Mon.- Sun.　12.00p - 4.00p
Or By Appointment

3464 Waialae Avenue
Between 9th & 10th
Honolulu, HI　96816
☎ 734-8869

Tom & Sweetie Moffatt (owner)
Tom Moffatt has presented over five decades of rock concerts from the Rolling Stones and Michael Jackson to Elton John (interspersed with performers from Sinatra to the Bolshoi) and now hosts a daily morning drive show on 107.9 FM. But he's only one half of a "Classic Couple." As a dancer touring the world and cultural ambassador of the islands, Sweetie made friends with ladies from Milan to Manhattan. Soon her global acquaintances began sending her their once-worn fashions, available to you now at Comme Ci Comme Ca.

CALICO GENERAL STORE

COUNTRY-STYLE GENERAL STORE

Calico General Store celebrates the spirit of an old-fashioned, small-town American country store. The instant you walk through the door you feel you're just a few steps away from the "Little House on the Prairie." We offer everything from calico sun bonnets to coonskin caps; from pikake/jasmine perfume to Hawaiian Passion Fire Sauce; from cuddly bears and rag dolls to spinning tops and yo-yo's! Owner Dawn Krause feels that "Hawaii has the best customers in the world. People come here to have a good time and we like to think of our store as part of the entertainment." So c'mon down for some good old homespun fun!

*The Spirit of
American Style*

Dawn Krause (owner)
"I love being in my store. It's a wonderful, creative outlet for me. But you know the saying, 'All work and no play. . . ' When I'm not working in the shop or enjoying a glass of wine with family and friends, I can usually be found swimming at the Central YMCA pool."

Mon.- Sat. 9.00a - 9.00p
Sunday   9.00a - 6.00p

Aloha Tower Market Place
Honolulu, HI 96813
☎ 524-0964

Map4 / D4 (AT) **27**

OPAL FIELDS

FINE JEWELRY & GEMS

Opal Fields is a full-service fine jewelry store specializing in striking, one-of-a-kind jewelry made from the rare and exotic black opal from Queensland, Australia. You'll also find other rare gems, natural mineral specimens, and fine Hawaiian wood art pieces in a museum-like setting.

* More than black opal *

Mon.- Fri. 10.30a - 8.00p
Saturday 11.30a - 8.00p

Restaurant Row, Ste 4D
Honolulu, Hawaii 96813
☎ 538-OPAL (6725)

http://www.opalfields.com

Thomas Wheeler (owner)
Tom is an American Gem
Society Certified Gemologist
Appraiser and an award-win-
ning jewelry designer and
goldsmith.

ISLAND PROVISION CO. AT VAGABOND HOUSE

FOR ISLAND LIVING

LM

Inspired by Hawaii poet Don Blanding's "Vagabond's House", the store is a relaxed, welcoming environment with one-of-a-kind items from Hawaii, the Pacific Rim, and around the world. In a home-like setting—with dining room, pantry, living room, bedroom, bath and garden areas—limited-edition handcrafted treasures share space with finds from the owner's travels.

Find your way home.

The Vagabonds:
Patty Kincaid, Kathy Merrill, Mary Philpotts & Daphne Chu. "We stepped back in time for inspiration, drawing upon Hawaii's unique history and multi-ethnic traditions."

Mon.- Sat.   10.00a - 9.00p
Sunday   10.00a - 5.00p

Ward Centre
Honolulu, HI 96814
☎ 593-0288

Map4 / D5 (W2) **29**

BookEnds

Why go to town when the best beaches on Oʻahu, fabulous restaurants, juice bars, ice cream shoppes, coffee hangouts, eclectic boutiques, and now, a real bookstore, are all in Kailua? BookEnds is for lingering, browsing, and in-store reading. A super-sized store we're not—but when you live in a small town on an island, small is beautiful. We're a booklovers' bookstore, filled with character and characters. Spend some time at BookEnds and you'll always walk out with a good story...

*A place
for books
in Kailua*

Mon.- Fri.   9.00a - 8.00p
Sat.- Sun.   9.00a - 5.00p

590 Kailua Road
Kailua, Hawaii, 96734
☎ 261-1996

Maile, Pat & Hans
We love books—we *really* love books! Hans is a graphic designer and artist with a soft spot for type, Pat has had a 25-year love affair with the written word and still can't get enough, and Maile's grateful the employee discount on books extends to owners.

CRAZY SHIRTS

SPORTSWEAR & RELATED APPAREL & ACCESSORIES

Remodeled and expanded to 2,000 sq. ft. in 1994, the International Market Place store on Kalakaua Avenue is the biggest, busiest, and highest in sales of the company's 50+ stores. What has kept Crazy Shirts ahead of its many imitators is Rick Ralston's ongoing passion for quality and innovation. He pioneered the design of shirts to his own demanding specifications, he continues to approve every design before it goes into produc-tion, and he maintains marketing and image control over all stores.

Rick Ralston (founder)

...began airbrushing designs on sweatshirts and T-shirts on the sidewalks of Waikiki in 1962. In 1964, he opened Ricky's Crazy Shirts in the back of International Market Place. Becoming Crazy Shirts Inc. two years later, the company still designs, manufactures, and markets its own exclusive brand of imprinted and embroidered sportswear and related apparel and accessories in Crazy Shirts shops throughout the Hawaiian Islands, Guam, the Mainland, and internationally through the Catalog Store and Internet Store for mail order customers.

Mon.- Sun.   8.00a - 11.30p

International Market Place
2332 Kalakaua Avenue
Waikiki, HI 96815
☎ 922-4791

Map2 / B1 **31**

FIRE IT UP!

Fire It Up! is a creative playground for the Picasso in all of us, offering one of the hottest new activities in town. This delightful activity inspires all ages to try their hand at creating one-of-a-kind ceramic designs. Choose from a wide variety of ceramic pieces and glaze colors, and paint to your heart's content—we do the rest. Whether you want to create a special gift, throw a unique party, or just escape the stress of modern-day living, Fire It Up! may be just the ticket. Come on in and find your artistic self. Personal and friendly staff await you.

The art of having fun

Carolyn & Colleen Hall (owners)
As partners, the twins share in the excitement and artistic pleasure of owning and managing a business in their home town of Honolulu. Their professional attitude, combined with an easy-going island style, makes the Fire It Up! experience something to remember and come back to time and again.

Sun.- Mon.   11.00a - 7.00p
Tue.- Sat.   11.00a - 8.00p

3045 Monsarrat Avenue
Honolulu, HI 96815
☎ 924-4444

Blue Hawaii Surf

Surfboards & Accessories

Top professional surfers around the world ride Blue Hawaii surfboards. Along with some of the best surfboards in the water, Blue Hawaii also carries quality apparel and accessories by all major surf brands. So when you think of surf, drop by Blue Hawaii, where surfing comes first.

Surf first!

Todd, Paul (owner), Michael (owner), Jaime & Rod
Established in 1984, Blue Hawaii Surf, featuring the work of shapers like Glen Minami and Mike Woo, has remained one of Hawaii's "core" surf shops.

Mon.- Sat.   9.00a - 9.00p
Sunday   9.00a - 5.00p

1446 Kona Street
Honolulu, HI 96814
☎ 943-2583

Map4 / D6 **33**

NEEDLEPOINT ETC.

NEEDLEPOINT SUPPLIES & INSTRUCTIONS

Needlepoint Etc. has everything for your needlepoint project, from inspiration to completion: canvases, including handpainted Hawaiian, tropical, Oriental, and Christmas themes or custom designs; fibers and threads; stitching hints; all the right tools; and classes, both individual and group.

The complete needlepoint shop

Tuesday 10.00a - 5.00p
Wednes. 10.00a - 7.00p
Thu.- Fri. 10.00a - 5.00p
Saturday 10.00a - 4.00p

2863 Kihei Place
Honolulu, HI 96816
☎ 737-3944

Louise "Gussie" Schubert (owner)
Stitching is a passion with me. I love to create wonderful works of art that I wear, use in my house, or give as gifts. Each project is an experience I love to share with others who want to stitch. Come in and see me!

HAWAIIAN HEIRLOOM JEWELRY FACTORY & MUSEUM

BY PHILIP RICKARD

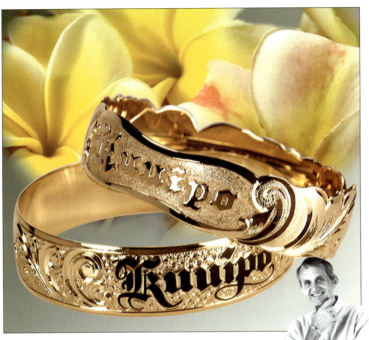

Our factory and museum is the home of the beloved and beautiful local jewelry made in Hawaii for over 130 years. Here the only authorized, authentic reproductions of the original Hoomanao Mau (A Lasting Remembrance) and the Aloha Oe (Queen Lili'uokalani's beautiful song of parting) bracelets are made in exacting detail. Our small, beautifully appointed museum traces the evolution and history of Hawaiian Heirloom Jewelry.

Behind the extensive showroom you can watch jewelry being manufactured daily— on a one-to-two-day completion basis—in our factory. Our book "Hawaiian Heirloom Jewelry: A Lasting Remembrance" details the history of the beautiful island jewelry and is available in bookstores and in our showroom.

Every piece a masterpiece

Philip Rickard (owner)
After years of manufacturing jewelry, Rickard started this business Jan. 1, 1986, with the intent to "depict the inherent Aloha Spirit in Hawaiian Jewelry and elevate it to a class of its own through excellence in craftsmanship and design." Today he focuses on representing the jewelry worldwide, since "everyone wants to be connected to Hawaii in some way, and the jewelry itself is a visual representation of that magic."

Mon.- Sun. 9.00a - 11.00p

Royal Hawaiian Shopping Ctr.
2301 Kalakaua Ave. C-306
Honolulu, HI 96815
☎ 924-7972

Map2 / B1 (RH) **35**

NATIVE BOOKS & BEAUTIFUL THINGS

LOCAL ARTISTS' COOPERATIVE

"So where can I buy something that's really made in Hawaii?" Go where the locals go, to "Native Books and Beautiful Things". We have two locations—one an oasis in downtown Honolulu, the other just inside the entrance to Bishop Museum. What you'll find at both is a beautifully displayed collection of handmade—by one of the 20 pairs of hands that owns the place—seed and shell lei, lauhala hats and bags, bamboo-stamped and quilt- and tattoo-inspired clothing, mu'umu'u, aloha shirts, holoholo slippers, colorful pareo, hula instruments, native plants and flowers interpreted in silver and gold, stone and wood, decorated ipu, homemade jams and jellies, and the best Na Mea Hawai'i books in town. It's an ever-changing collection, all made right here in the middle of the Pacific Ocean.

Really made in Hawaii

Mon.- Fri.   8.00a - 5.00p
Saturday   9.00a - 4.00p
Bishop Museum 7 days 9 to 5

222 Merchant Street
Honolulu, Hawaii, 96813
☎ 599-5511

A Few Of Our 'Ohana... People are surprised that a hui of 20 artists owns the store. How do we do it? Hawaiian style—everybody works for the good of the group. We live on an island, where the only way to live is working together.

NEWT AT THE ROYAL

MEN'S & WOMEN'S APPAREL

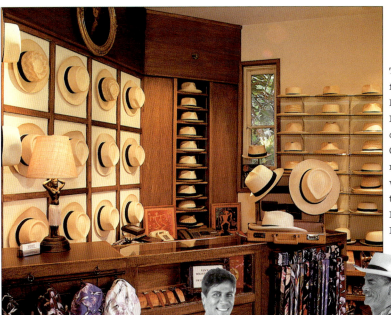

G H

This exclusive little shop features the legendary handcrafted Montecristi Panama Hats. These classically styled Fedoras, Optimos and Plantations for men and women are hand-woven by the artisans of the town of Montecristi, Ecuador. American Presidents, European and Asian royalty, Hollywood stars, famous writers, and great sportsmen all have sought out these rare fashion treasures. Newt also has Hawaiian Retro Print Tropical Shirts, with exclusive patterns adapted from popular designs of the '40s & '50s. Each shirt, carefully cut and sewn in our own workshop.

Legendary Panama Hats

Tom Souza & Fred Newton (proprietor) Newt continues the island tradition of the Aloha shirt, which dates back to the early '30s, when Ellery J. Chun began selling shirts in his small King-Smith Clothiers shop in Honolulu.

Mon.- Sat.   8.30a - 9.30p

2259 Kalakaua Avenue
at Royal Hawaiian Hotel
Honolulu, HI 96815
☎ 808-922-0062

1-800-508-HATS

Map2 / B1 **37**

NAISH HAWAII LTD.

WINDSURFING WHOLESALE, RETAIL, REPAIR, RENTAL & LESSONS

Kailua Bay is an ideal place to learn to wind-surf. The Naish school has taught thousands of people basic through advanced skills. Professional instructors provide personal attention, including instruction in several languages. Excellent rental equipment is available for all skill levels. The retail shop features Naish sails and Naish-designed boards, with the largest selection of new and used windsurfing equipment on the island. There's also a great selection of Naish T-shirts and accessories, windsurfing videos and magazines—and anything else you need to get out on the water and WINDSURF.

*Windsurf
with the
pros*

Mon.- Sun.   9.00a - 5.30p

155 Hamakua Drive
Kailua, HI 96734
☎ 262-6068

Fax 263-9723

Carol Naish

In 1976 Robby Naish won his first Wind-surfing World Championship at the age of 13. His dad, Rick, turned the family garage into a workshop, building boards for himself and sons Randy and Robby. As the Naishes' reputation grew, more and more people wanted Rick's boards. In 1979, Rick and his wife Carol opened the first "Naish Hawaii" shop in Kailua. Today, Robby is still one of the top competitive sailors in the world. Rick continues to design highly-rated boards for the international market, with new models coming out each year. Carol manages the business.

MARSHA NADALIN SALON

FULL-SERVICE SALON & DAY SPA

Marsha Nadalin Salon is proud of its reputation as the area's finest full-service salon. With emphasis on ongoing education and new product knowledge for the entire staff, Marsha Nadalin Salon is able to meet your most discriminating demands. The accent is on beautiful, healthy-looking hair, styled in the latest and most distinctive fashion, with variations to suit your individual personality.

Feel great about the way you look after every visit

Marsha & managing team Joy & Michele

Conveniently located in the prestigious Kahala Mall, the salon first opened for business at this location in 1993 and has since provided the most up to date professional and personalized services to both men and women.

Mon.- Fri.	9.00a - 9.00p
Saturday	9.00a - 8.00p
Sunday	10.00a - 5.00p

Kahala Mall
Honolulu, HI 96816
☎ 737-8505

Map2 / D3 (KM) **39**

THE UKULELE HOUSE

WHERE UKULELES LIVE

G·H

Hawaii's newest ukulele shop offers the largest selection of new and vintage ukuleles in Honolulu. We have ukuleles to fit every budget and for every level of enthusiast, from beginners to collectors. Brands include Kelii, Koaloha, Braddah, and fine vintage instruments from Kamaka, C.F. Martin, and Gibson. From strings and cases to songbooks and aloha shirts, anything to do with the ukulele can be found here.

*Promoting Hawaiian
culture through
the ukulele*

Osamu & Daniel
The ukulele has always been a part of the Hawaiian lifestyle. Everyone has had a good time with the ukulele— listening to an uncle playing at a beach party or just strumming along with songs on the radio. At the Ukulele House, ukuleles are finally getting the recognition they deserve.

Mon.- Fri. 10.00a - 4.00p
Saturday 10.00a - 2.00p

331-B Kamani Street
Honolulu, HI 96813
☎ 593-8587

HAWAIIAN RUGS™

Indich Collection is proud to present Hawaiian Rugs™, the natural evolution of fine Oriental rug making. Ideal for island living and inspired by our rich flora and fauna, these Hawaiian Heritage rugs are designed by local artists and then hand-crafted by master weavers in Nepal, using exacting standards, fabrics, and century-old techniques that have been passed down through generations. Nine signature designs are available in a range of tropical colors—or custom design your own for a true, one-of-a-kind interior sensation. Come see why Hawaiian Rugs™ have captured the imagination of designers, residents, and visitors alike— only at the Indich Collection!

Where Hawaii shops for fine Hawaiian and oriental rugs

Bill Indich (owner)

Whether for traditional Persian, Chinese, Kilims, or contemporary Hawaiian Rugs™, there's only one place to shop for designer rugs in Hawaii. "The balance between beautiful design, superior quality, and outstanding value is the key to buying fine rugs. That's why we back our rugs with a 100% guarantee. Our mission is to give our customers an array of choices to furnish their homes and offices. We know that every rug is as distinctive as its owner's personality."

Mon.- Sat. 9.30a - 5.30p
Sunday 10.00a - 4.00p

Gentry Pacific Design Ctr.
560 N. Nimitz Hwy, #101
Honolulu, HI 96817
☎ 524-7769

Map4 / C3 **41**

THE GROWING KEIKI

A UNIQUE CHILDREN'S SHOP

The Growing Keiki features an eclectic array of funky, fashionable clothing for infants and children (including 100% cotton items), books written and published locally, handmade wooden toys, and one-of-a-kind gifts for that someone special to cherish for a lifetime. The store's recipe for success is carefully chosen and often handcrafted specialty items, offered with aloha and excellent customer service. The Growing Keiki values its loyal local customers as well as our mainland regulars who return year after year.

To amuse & delight
the child in each of us

Nancy & Lee (owners)

Established in 1987, The Growing Keiki occupies a restored 1930s building in historic Haleiwa Town. Owners Nancy M. Woolley and Lee Brooke Roy, both mothers of twins, live by their philosophy: "Do what you love, be of service to others, and never compromise comfort or quality." They invite you to make The Growing Keiki a part of your day during your next visit to Haleiwa, the most charming town on Oahu.

Mon.- Sat. 9.30a - 5.30p
Sunday   10.00a - 5.00p

66-051 Kam Hwy
Haleiwa, HI 96712
☎ 637-4544

KIM TAYLOR REECE
GALLERY

FINE ART PHOTOGRAPHY

The Kim Taylor Reece Gallery is located amid the lush green mountains and sparkling waters of windward Oahu. Created to share fine art photography in breathtaking surroundings, the gallery features handmade original works. Since 1978 Kim Taylor Reece has studied the hula kahiko to create an award-winning style that has helped to revive this ancient dance. Although hula was at one time banned for its "heathen" qualities of raw emotion and sexuality, Kim captures its grace, strength and beauty as only an artist can do. Reece says, "The beauty of our surroundings exemplifies what I am trying to create with the dance."

Passion, beauty, strength—Hula as it was meant to be

Kim Taylor Reece (artist)
Dancers can fly. They can soar. They can take you up to the heavens, through a raging lava flow, and out over an endless sea. Hula inspires, impassions, and awes the viewer. As an artist it has been my passion to capture, preserve, and share these feelings. I hope you find as much delight and inspiration in my work as I have had in creating it.

Mon.- Tue.   12.00p - 6.00p
Thu.-Sat.   12.00p - 6.00p
Wed. & Sun. Closed

53-866 Kamehameha Hwy
Sacred Falls, HI 96717
☎ 293-2000

Map3 / A1 43

HANG LOOSE JUICE

FRESH HAWAIIAN JUICE & SMOOTHIE BAR

Hang Loose Juice whips up a special blend of liquid energy from all-natural ingredients—Hawaiian style. Goodies like papaya, starfruit juice, mac nuts— even poi. Fresh veggies too! Cool off with smooth- ies and fresh-squeezed juices that fuel your engine and taste terrific!

GH

Juice up
your
taste buds,
Hawaiian style

Mon.- Fri. 6.30a - 6.00p
Saturday 8.00a - 2.00p

801 Alakea St. Ste 110
Honolulu, HI 96813
☎ 536-5667

Thomas Burke (owner)
Downsized out of a job at UH, Tom Burke decided to Hawaiianize the juice bar craze. He created some tasty sensations at home and now is busy making sure everyone "eats" their fruits and veggies with a big smile!

Other Realms

The Comic & Game Specialist

Step out of your everyday life and enter the fantastic worlds of Other Realms. Featuring a vast array of unique collectibles, adventure games, hobby supplies, and comic books, Other Realms is Hawaii's premier source of products that let your imagination run wild. Come explore. You'll find a friendly and knowledgeable staff, a treasure trove of merchandise, and ongoing events and special gaming activities.

Leave the world. Step into adventure

I am **Gunther**, otherwise known as "the cat" here at Other Realms. I watch over the place to make sure things get done. I also keep our customers informed about exciting product news and events. To my right is **Charles Whitesell**, the owner, who opened the shop ten years ago. On the other side is **Jeff Jacobson**, the general manager. His is the friendly face you are likely to see. Do give us a visit and let us show you Other Realms.

Mon.- Sat.   10.00a - 9.00p
Sunday   10.00a - 5.00p

Ward Warehouse #A1-30
Honolulu, HI 96814
☎ 596-8236

Map4 / D5 (W1)   45

PACIFIC ORIENT TRADERS INC.

ANTIQUES OF ASIA

Pacific Orient Traders, a source of antique furnishings directly imported from Asia, is pleased to present its first collection of Asian home furnishings at its newly opened Honolulu showroom. Each one-of-a-kind piece has been hand-selected and most are accompanied by a certificate of authenticity from the People's Republic of China. Most furnishings are over 100 years old and have been expertly refinished by Chinese craftsman. Choose from an impressive selection of armoirs, chests, cabinets, chairs, occasional tables, altar tables, sideboards, and very rare pieces such as opium beds and antique temple doors. All our prices reflect our direct whole-sale importation.

GH

Specializing in furniture direct from Asia at affordable prices

Shawn Krajchir (co-owner)
...and husband Richard have been in the import-export business for over 20 years, "to give people the opportunity to own a piece of the past at very affordable prices." At their 5,000-sq.-ft. showroom you will find no two pieces of furniture alike and a variety of original Asian antiques not found anywhere else in Hawaii.

Tue.- Sat.   9.30a - 4.30p
Sunday   10.00a - 3.00p

720 Iwilei Road, #222
Honolulu, HI 96817
☎ 531-3774

JEFF CHANG POTTERY & FINE CRAFTS

FINE CRAFTS GALLERY

Located on a landmark property in Kaneohe, in the previous home of the Honda family, the shop combines a fine crafts gallery with the atmosphere of an old-fashioned country store. Local residents and visitors who come to browse the always changing selections and buy one-of-a-kind gifts for others and themselves become friends who pull up a chair for a visit. Selections include Jeff's distinctive stoneware and Raku pottery and the works of more than 200 island and mainland artisans working in all craft media, including fine woodwork, blown glass and collectibles, art jewelry, fountains, mobiles, clocks, chimes, animal sculptures, musical instruments, lamps, Christmas ornaments, and mirrors.

From our hands to yours

Corey, Jeff & Karon
The Changs personally oper-ate the shop. Customer ser-vices include complimentary gift boxes, gift certificates, gift registry, layaway, and packing and shipping.

Mon.- Sun. 9.00a - 7.00p
Oct.-Dec.   9.00a - 9.00p

45-781B Kamehameha Hwy.
Kaneohe, HI 96744
☎ 235-2808

Map3 / B3 **47**

ROXY QUIKSILVER HONOLULU

BEACH AND CASUAL WEAR FOR WOMEN & GIRLS

Roxy Quiksilver Honolulu opened in 1996 as the first all-women's surf boutique in the world. Our store carries Roxy Quiksilver's Sportswear line, a classic, whimsical beachwear collection including T-shirts, boardshorts, dresses, swimwear, footwear, and more, directed toward active young women who know what they want! We also carry Teenie Wahine, Roxy's newly introduced children's line. Come and visit our friendly staff in the Ward Village Shops, across the street from Ward Centre.

**Fashionable &
functional
sportswear
for active young
women**

🌀
Mon.- Sat.10.00a - 9.00p
Sunday   10.00a - 7.00p

1116 Auahi St., Bay
#3 (Ward Village)
Honolulu, HI 96814
☎ 596-7699

Roxy Quiksilver Staff
Owners Jake Mizuno and Dane Kealoha are two avid watermen who have dedicated themselves to bringing their fellow waterwomen fashionable and functional clothing and accessories to fit their active lifestyles!

PATRIOTIC SPORTS

FASHION "CAMO" CLOTHING

L.M

At Patriotic Sports, the shopping headquarters for all your camouflage clothing and accessory needs, you will find tough, functional—and fashionable—military-style clothing and gear. We have something for everyone, any age or size. While you're here, don't forget your utility tools and knives. Give us a visit and you'll be surprised at how much we have to offer.

*Not just a store—
an adventure*

Tina (young adventurer)

Mon.- Sat. 9.00a - 9.00p
Sunday   9.00a - 6.00p

1 Aloha Tower Drive 249A
Honolulu, HI 96813
☎ 537-1818

Map4 / D4 (AT) **49**

FLYIN' HAWAIIAN BALLOONS

FULL-SERVICE BALLOON SHOP

Bubbly balloons, beautiful and bright! A
festival of colors—oh, what a sight! Flowers
and arches, columns and bouquets—all
made with balloons in a joyous way!
Celebrate today with these flights of fancy.
It will surely lift your spirits. At a price
that isn't fancy.

*Inflation
can
be fun!*

Tanya & Ken
(hot air crew)
Celebrating with Hawaii
Nei since 1983, Flyin'
Hawaiian Balloons pro-
vides full-service balloon
decor and balloon
deliveries for all occa-
sions, customized for
your event—creativity
& quality always at the
forefront.

Mon.- Fri.   8.00a - 6.00p
Saturday   8.30a - 6.00p
Sunday   by appointment

1133 South King Street
Honolulu, HI 96814
☎ 593-1774

1-800-731-1774

THE KITCHEN & SPICE CO.

SPICES, HERBS, TEAS, COFFEES, KITCHEN ACCESSORIES & GOURMET FOODS

This is not just a store, it's an experience! As you enter, the essence of over 400 spices and herbs tantalizes your senses. We also have over 150 teas from around the globe, and a vast array of coffees, packaged gourmet foods, and kitchen utensils. The owner's passion for cooking will shine through as she answers your questions and caters to your every need.

Isn't it time to spice up your life?

Linda Gehring (owner)
Linda and husband Ted (of Teddy's Bigger Burgers—also on Monsarrat Ave.) started the Kitchen & Spice Co. to fill the need for high-quality, yet fairly priced spices and teas. In her spare time, Linda enjoys ocean sports, such as kayaking, paddling, and surfing.

Mon.- Sat.   11.00a - 8.00p
Sunday   11.00a - 7.00p

3045 Monsarrat Ave, Ste. 7
Honolulu, HI 96815
☎ 735-6393

Map2 / C1 **51**

QUILTS HAWAII

HOME OF QUALITY COMFORTERS, PLUS

A "made in Hawaii" store specializing in quilted comforters, shams, pillowcases, and a complete line of Hawaiian infant accessories. We also offer expandable bags, overnight sleeping bags with comforters, convertible rag caps, and games, including our exclusive Pipeline and Jan Ken Po cards. You'll also find treasured Hawaiian hand quilts from yesteryear, authentic sculptured bone and ivory jewelry, and other fine gift items.

*Bring the
tropical
outdoors in*

Mon.- Sat.   9.00a - 5.30p

2338 South King Street
Honolulu, HI 96826
☎ 942-3195

Leone (owner/designer)
Hawaiiana appraiser, designer, and active educator/supporter of Hawaiian artistry and culture, Leone Kamana Okamura, also known as Puamae'ole, has been declared a "Living Treasure" by the State of Hawaii.

RALSTON ANTIQUES & COLLECTIBLES

ANTIQUES

G H

An intriguing array of nostalgia is what you'll find at Ralston Antiques & Collectibles. The store is stocked with everything from traditional antique furniture to old toys, whaling artifacts, and Hawaiiana—all the things Rick Ralston personally loves and collects. The treasures are displayed in and on antique cabinets and tables, including massive merchandise cases purchased from a long-gone Chicago department store. Look for a diverse selection of clocks, silver, quilts, paintings, weapons, lamps, bronzes, ship models, scrimshaw, sculpture, golf memorabilia, and jewelry. The only qualifications for including items is that they must be high-quality and unusual.

Hervé Montagné (mgr.)
Gallery owner Rick Ralston is an avid collector specializing in antique toys. In 1994 Ralston published his own 324-page guide called *Cast Iron Floor Trains*, the most complete volume ever published on these collectibles. This beautiful coffee-table book identifies every locomotive and car known to exist and includes a rarity and price guide.

Wed.- Sun.   10.30a - 6.00p

66-030 Kam Highway
Haleiwa, HI 96712
☎ 637-8837
1-800-486-9794

Map1 / B2 **53**

BOUTIQUE APROPOS

SPECIALTY CLOTHING & ACCESSORIES

Boutique Apropos (apropos means "suitable, appropriate, befitting") features a diverse and exciting collection of designer labels from all over the world, including Cosabella from Italy, Morgan De Toi from France, Dr. Martens from the U.K., and Parasuco Sportswear from Canada. You'll find bodywear, sportswear, shoes, dresses, and accessories, attractively displayed and at a range of prices to fit your budget.

Apropos!

Mon.- Sat.   10.00a - 9.00p
Sunday   10.00a - 5.00p

Kahala Mall
Honolulu, HI 96816
☎ 735-1611

Minou (owner)
Minou owned several designer boutiques in Germany before moving to Oahu in 1983. Her first Hawaii store was in Waikiki, but she closed it and her European stores to concentrate on her Kahala Mall store, with its happy mix of local customers and tourists. Those customers love the unique, lightweight, and body-beautiful clothing "apropos for Hawaii."

VIN GLACE

FINE CANADIAN ICEWINES

Icewine, produced under exacting conditions in which grapes are allowed to freeze on the vine, is nature's gift to the wine lover. Icewine's intense natural sweetness, highly aromatic bouquet, and depth of flavors are without equal among dessert wines. Vin Glace is the only store in the world dedicated exclusively to the sale of Icewines and the only store in Hawaii contracted to sell the world's finest Icewines.

*Fight global warming.
Drink Icewine*

Glenn Murakami (owner)
"I've always been bored doing the same thing, and my business history reflects that wanderlust and restlessness. I've been involved in various enterprises, from music to telecommunications, from being a lawyer to baking cookies. But starting Vin Glace and creating a showcase for a truly unique and extraordinary libation has been a real kick.

Mon.- Sat.   9.00a - 9.00p
Sunday   9.00a - 6.00p

Aloha Tower Marketplace, 2nd Fl.
Honolulu, HI 96813
☎ 808-538-6399 Fax 808-373-5382

Map4 / D4 (AT) **55**

SIAM IMPORTS

TREASURES FROM THAILAND

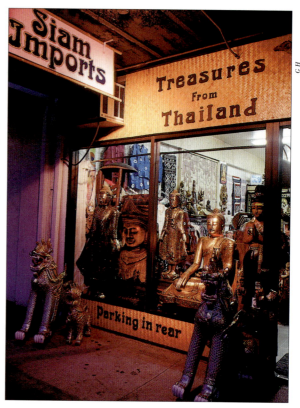

Shopping at the famous Chiang Mai Night Market in Thailand is a legendary experience — and now, the night market shopping experience is yours, right here in Honolulu, at Siam Imports. Kevin Costello's years of travel to Thailand have enabled him to put together the finest collection of clothing, jewelry, tapestries, sculptures, furniture, and much, much more! The shop's location, next to the Moʻiliʻili Community Center, where different cultures blend, is ideal for displaying unique, high-quality Thai handicrafts. For wholesale & mail orders please call 1-888-475-2255 (toll free), or email us at iamsiam@mci2000.com Remember, for bargains and excitement, come to Siam Imports, at 2567 South King St. (next to Kinko's). Open daily, 9am to 8pm, or call at 951-SIAM.

*We bring
Thailand
to you!*

Mon.- Sun. 9.00a - 8.00p

2567 South King St.
Honolulu, HI 96826
☎ 951-SIAM (7426)

Saengdao Costello
Shop owners Kevin and Saengdao Costello offer warm and gracious Thai hospitality, along with knowledge of Thailand, Saengdao's homeland.

Oahu Homebrew Supply

Beer And Wine-Making Supplies

If you like microbrews— handcrafted beers prepared in small batches at regional breweries—then you'll love the handcrafted beers you can make in your own home. Fresh malted grains, aromatic hops, and classic yeast strains in abundant varieties open up endless possibilities for your own unique brew. If you think malted barley will smell good simmering on your stove, just wait 'til you add the hops!

Oahu Homebrew Crew Mark and Cathy Scheitlin started brewing beer with a kit they received as a gift. Now they're proud to share their passion with other beer enthusiasts. By offering quality equipment, fresh ingredients, informative books, and brewing advice, Mark and Cathy hope their customers will never again have to settle for a mass-produced beer.

* Just brew it! *

Mon.- Fri.   10.30a - 6.30p
Saturday   10.00a - 5.00p

856 Ilaniwai St. #103
Honolulu, HI 96813
☎ 596-BREW (2739)

Map4 / D5 **57**

LEONARD'S BAKERY

HOME OF MALASADAS & PAO DOCE

What's the first thing that comes to mind when malasadas are mentioned? Why Leonard's Bakery, of course! Those melt-in-your-mouth Portuguese doughnuts have made Leonard's a household name. Leonard's, for quality, service and cleanliness.

LM

* The first & finest name in malasadas *

Sun.- Thu.   6.00a - 9.00p
Fri.- Sat.   6.00a - 10.00p

933 Kapahulu Avenue
Honolulu, Hi 96816
☎ 737-5591

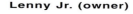

Lenny Jr. (owner)
Leonard's was started in 1952 by Leonard Rego, a local boy from Wailuku, Maui, and his wife, Margaret. Today, Leonard Jr. continues to sell quality products with friendly, efficient service. "Perhaps one day my son will want to fill the shoes I leave behind. I only hope they'll be as big as the ones my father left me." At only one and a half years old, little Leonard III has a long way to go before he's ready to run the family business, but he already loves malasadas, and for that matter, his father's big shoes!

POMEGRANATES IN THE SUN

W O M E N ' S   C L O T H I N G   &   A C C E S S O R I E S

Artful and delightfully exotic, Pomegranates In The Sun has been defining Pacific Rim fashion for 15 years. Trained staff will advise you on accessories and alterations, so even your off-the-rack outfit will have a style that is uniquely yours!

* Pacific Rim Fashions for our relaxed & wonderfully unique island lifestyle*

Jill with Joelle, Tiffany, Gabriella & Rachel
Pomegranates In The Sun serves as the showcase for Jill's colorful, made-in-Hawaii clothing line, which is catching on—both island-wide and nationally. She also brings an eclectic array of clothing and accessories from her travels around the world.

Mon.- Sat.	10.00a - 9.00p
Sunday	10.00a - 5.00p

Ward Warehouse
Honolulu, HI 96814
☎ 591-2208

Map4 / D5 (W1) **59**

MᶜCLAIN AUCTIONS

A U C T I O N S ,   A N T I Q U E S   &   M O R E !

The Ultimate Attic is Hawaii's largest antique store and the home of Hawaii's #1 full-service auction company. Bikes and boats hang from the ceiling; lamps, vases, and treasure chests are propped up on desks, chairs and tables; pillows are tossed on couches; framed paintings cover the walls. Repair, restoration, and reupholstery services are also available. Come travel back in time, explore, and enjoy.

A whole lot more than just another store

Tue.- Sat.   9.00a - 5.00p

825 Halekauwila Street
Honolulu, HI 96813
☎ 538-7227

Marty McClain (owner)
McClain Auctions, Hawaii's answer to the big mainland and European auction houses, has conducted auctions in Hawaii and the Pacific Basin for over 20 years—auctioning everything from large local estates to jewelry, fine art, antiques, and Hawaiiana. We pride ourselves on providing the best possible service to both sellers and buyers.

ORII DESIGNS

WOMEN'S & CHILDREN'S CLOTHING

Our women's and children's apparel features Tetsuo Orii's original designs, including beautiful flower lei T-shirts and other items inspired by the Aloha Spirit he has come to know in the islands.

Designer apparel at affordable prices

Tetsuo Leo Orii (owner)
Tetsuo Leo Orii was born in Manchuria near the Russian border in 1937. He returned to Japan at age 9 at the end of WWII. In 1962 he opened his own studio in Hawaii designing and manufacturing custom wall tapestries and, later, fossil stone furnishings.
His former clientele include:
- **former President Richard Nixon**
- **King Hussein**
- **Bjorn Borg**
- **Carol Burnett**
- **Bruce Jenner**
- **Martina Navratilova**
- **and many more.**

Mon.- Sat.   12.00p - 10.00p
Sunday   3.00p - 10.00p

2310 Kuhio Avenue #5
Honolulu, HI 96815
☎ 922-1007

Map2 / B1 **61**

NAKEʻU AWAI DESIGNS

HAWAIIAN-STYLE FASHIONS/ISLAND MOTIF FABRICS

A creative spirit with flair, Nakeʻu Awai designs Hawaiian-style fashions for the local market using fabric silk-screened by hand with commissioned art work as well as art of his own design. Come see—and feel—his beautiful clothing for men, women, and children.

Nakeʻu Awai Designs— a layering of textures

Call For Appointment

1613 Houghtailing #5
Honolulu, HI 96817
☎ 808-841-1221

Nakeʻu Awai (owner/designer) A graduate of the Kamehameha Schools and the University of Washington, Nakeʻu Awai has been a dancer on stage and television productions. While residing in L.A. as a performer, he began handcrafting macrame creations for such celebrities as Lena Horne, Goldie Hawn and Elvis Presley. Nakeʻu returned home to Oahu in the early 1970s and resolved to make a statement about fashion in Hawaii. He has made his influence felt and attributes some of his success to a determined attitude. Today he enjoys a prominent place among Hawaii's textile and clothing designers.

RUSS·K MAKAHA

LONGBOARD SURF SHOP

We specialize in surfboards from 8 feet to 12 feet, meshing high performance with classic style. We offer custom longboard shapes from Hawaii's top surfboard shapers; fabric inlays, pigmented resin, and multiple stringer boards; cutting-edge fin design from F.C.S.; wingnut, manta, and barracuda skegs; Quiksilver, Roxy, Da Hui, and Makaha T-Shirts. We also specialize in surfwear and accessories exclusively made in Hawaii, including silver jewelry, souvenir Balsawood longboards, and keychains.

Hawaii's longboard headquarters

Rusty and Sunny

Russ K Keaulana captured longboard's most prestigious title 3 years in a row, dominating the sport from 1993 to 1995. Russ, son of renowned waterman, lifeguard, and champion surfer Buffalo Keaulana, operates the Russ K shop with his wife Sunny— daughter of legendary Sunset surfer Barry Kanaiaupuni—and partner Craig Inouye.

Mon.- Fri. 10.00a - 8.00p
Saturday 10.00a - 7.00p
Sunday 10.00a - 6.00p

1695 Kapiolani Blvd. #C
Honolulu, HI 96814
☎ 951-7877

Map2 / A1 **63**

HONOLULU WORKOUT CO.

WORKOUTWEAR, ACTIVEWEAR & DANCEWEAR

Unique. Exciting. Invigorating. Our store motivates you to work out, get in shape, and look great in quality basics to mix and match. We stock men's, women's, and children's workoutwear, activewear, swimwear, dancewear, and dance shoes. Our dance shoes include ballet, pointe, jazz, and tap.

Fashion for your active lifestyle

Mon.- Fri.	10.00a - 7.30p
Saturday	9.00a - 7.30p
Sunday	11.00a - 5.00p

Family Sports Center
1020 Auahi St. Bldg #8
Honolulu, HI 96814
☎ 597-8004

Debi Ozawa (owner)

Debi is a former Miss Waikiki and Sheraton Hotels Poster Girl. Her fitness lifestyle includes running, fitness kickboxing, ballet barre class, swimming, and rollerblading, and her goal is to motivate others to join her in getting and staying fit.

THE PACIFIC HOBBYIST

PLASTIC MODEL SHOP

We are the ultimate store for the plastic model hobbyist. Because model building has changed dramatically over the years, many adults who built models as kids are shocked and sometimes overwhelmed by the number of products available. With our knowledge and expertise, we can help advanced modelers or beginners—no matter what age— have fun and enjoy making something with their own hands.

A scale model is a challenge to build

Owen, Brad & Ken (owners)

Mon.- Sat.   10.00a - 6.00p
Sunday   12.00p - 5.00p

2015 South King Street
Honolulu, HI 96826
☎ 942-2851 Fax 945-3091

Map2 / A2 **65**

MONTSUKI

KIMONO • INSPIRED DESIGNER APPAREL

With simplicity and elegance, from traditional to contemporary—this is what Montsuki clothing designs are about. An independent self-made Hawaii business, we design innovative clothing by transforming vintage silk kimonos and obis into stylish, wearable apparel.

* Reflect your individuality *

Patty & Janet (owners)
My mother and I started our business in August 1979, with a small inventory of kimonos, obis, and fabrics. Our business grew, usually by word of mouth from customers' referrals. We truly appreciate our clientele, some of whom have been with us since those early years. I always say, "If it were not for them—our customers—we could never have attained our dream."

Mon.- Sat.   9.30a - 4.00p

1148 Koko Head Avenue
Honolulu, Hi 96816
☎ 734-3457

RICHES KAHALA

H IGH F ASHION A CCESSORIES

L.M

Savvy islanders know that when they see a fabulous accessory on the editorial pages of Elle or Vogue the exclusive place to find it is Riches Kahala. This oasis of sophisticated style is the best-kept secret in the city. Riches breaks through the desert of sameness to bring its dedicated customers an eclectic collection of handbags, hats, gifts, and jewelry—from faux to fine, glitz to glamour, serious to whimsical, with prices to please every pocketbook: $20 to $2,000. Lo and Clyde Kaimuloa are clearly on the cutting edge of fashion, ahead of the trends. Kate Spade, Lunch at the Ritz, Sequoia, Seno, and Bettina Duncan are just a few of the designers introduced to the islands by Riches.

*He nani mai loko aku.
Beauty from the inside out*

Clyde & Lo (owners)
The Kaimuloas search the globe for the best of everything. Homegrown designers share the Riches treasure chest with collections from Italy, France, Israel, New York, Samoa, Japan, and Tahiti.

Mon.- Sat.   10.00a - 9.00p
Sunday   10.00a - 5.00p

Kahala Mall
Honolulu, HI 96816
☎ 737-3303

Map2 / D3 (KM) **67**

OUT OF THE WEST

WESTERN WEAR & ACCESSORIES

The westernmost western wear shop in the United States, Out of the West offers an extensive line of western clothing, accessories, jewelry, and gifts. Featured brands include Tony Lama, Double-D Ranchwear, Saddle Ridge, Montana Silver Smiths, Crum Line, Desert West, Justin, Stetson, and Wrangler (the real cowboy's choice).

Only the best in western wear

Mark & Greg Davies (owners)
With over 30 years in Hawaii retailing experience, brothers Mark and Greg have long shared a love of horses, western folklore, and the cowboy mystique.

Mon.- Sat.   9.00a - 9.00p
Sunday   9.00a - 6.00p

Aloha Tower Marketplace
Honolulu, HI 96813
☎ 521-5552

BISHOP MUSEUM SHOPS

MUSEUM GIFT SHOPS

Shop Pacifica features Hawaiian and South Pacific books, Hawaiian language and music products, and one-of-a-kind handcrafted gift items made by Hawaiian and South Pacific Artisans. The Castle Discovery Shop features educational products related to current Museum exhibits. Products of note include: astronaut food, pens, posters, and an array of space exploration CD-ROMs and videos. Other items sure to stir the imagination include prehistoric animal replicas, mineral rocks, and numerous "How to" kits.

Linking knowledge & people for a better future

A Few Of The Museum Ohana

Bishop Museum, the State Museum of Natural and Cultural History, is one of the world's leading scientific institutions. Named for Bernice Pauahi, a Hawaiian princess who married Charles Reed Bishop, a Caucasian commoner, the museum houses Bernice's magnificent collection of Hawaiian artifacts.

Mon.- Sun.   9.00a - 5.00p
except xmas day

1525 Bernice Street
Honolulu, HI 96817
☎ 848-4158

Map4 / B2 **69**

OCEANS IN GLASS

ART FROM THE DEPTHS OF SOUL & SEA

At Oceans in Glass Gallery, Krista Woodward (one of three sisters (all practicing, successful artists!) is reviving the classic art of "flamework" sculpting. By manipulating rods of glass in intense flame, the sculptor's concentration and patent mastery bring to life the distinctive shapes and outrageous colors of Hawaii's vivid marine riches. Krista's creative gift and refined color work has attracted other glass masters to display with her. The gallery takes pride in representing only museum quality glass art. So, when you've found that perfect gleaming dolphin or matched set of spirited reef fish, your treasure will be placed in specifically designed wrapping guaranteed to help safeguard your Island purchase during your trip home.

*Presenting ocean art
at its exquisite best!*

Krista Woodward & George Atkins
"Check out the lack of bubbles—a sign of true ability," says owner and delighted father, George Atkins. "Krista is one of the best in the world employing predictable color on a larger scale. People love working with her on their custom art glass commissions."

Mon.- Sun. 10.00a - 7.00p

North Shore Marketplace
66-250 Kam Hwy
Haleiwa, HI 96712
☎ 637-3366

ISLAND GUITARS

MUSICAL INSTRUMENTS, NEW, USED & VINTAGE

We are a bunch of fun-loving guys who also love guitars. We offer unparalleled service based on years of experience buying, selling, trading, and repairing musical instruments. Our inventory of well over 500 instruments includes a wide selection of the finest new and vintage instruments on the market. No high pressure sales here. We sell only what we believe in and would be proud to have in our personal collections.

*Great guitars
of the past—the
finest instruments
of today*

John, Douglas, Neil, Peter & Jim (not shown) -- crew Island Guitars opened its doors in 1984 on N. King St. as a small store dedicated to the sales and service of used and vintage instruments. On opening day, there were only 5 guitars on the wall! Fifteen years later, we're the largest guitar store in Hawaii.

Mon.- Sat.   10.00a - 9.00p
Sunday   10.00a - 5.00p

Ward Warehouse
Honolulu, HI 96814
☎ 591-2910

Map4 / D5 (W1) **71**

MANUHEALIʻI

DESIGN, MANUFACTURE & RETAIL OF HAWAIIAN APPAREL

The Manuhealiʻi Collection captures the essence of Aloha attire, mixing original Hawaiian quilt patterns with contemporary colors and styles to create a line of cool, comfortable, and stylish clothing for the whole family. Visit our gallery, located on the windward side of Oʻahu, in Kailua town—only minutes from the award-winning Kailua Beach.

Distinctly Hawaiian... uniquely Manuhealiʻi

Tue.- Fri.   9.30a - 5.30p
Saturday   9.00a - 4.00p
Sunday   9.00a - 1.00p

629 Kailua Road #104A
Kailua, HI 96734
☎ 261-9865

Danene & Pono (owners)
Pono and Danene Lunn are the architect/fashion designer team behind Manuhealiʻi Inc. Both local products have been married since 1983 and are the parents of three young men. They delight in the challenges of each successive step in building a business. Pono and Danene continue to create a collection of original and stylish designs with an ever-changing palette of colors for the contemporary Hawaiian.

OUTRIGGER TRADING CO.

FINE GIFTS & COLLECTIBLES

Haleiwa offers the unique combination of historic city, interesting people, beautiful mountains, ocean views, and unforgettable sunsets. This one-day getaway from Honolulu becomes more of a treat when you visit Outrigger Trading Co. Our "mix" is unpretentious and simple: the work of local artisans and cottage-industry individuals—collectible and practical items with a tropical flair. For non-shoppers, we offer a comfortable koa bench from which to view the dramatic Kaena Point coastline and, as a final treat, five tempting flavors of home-made fudge!

A shop with something for everyone

Debbie Ahern (owner)
I still maintain a title within my family dating back to grade school—Best Shopper! For every birthday, holiday, or celebration, I was asked to pick out something "just right" and certain to please the recipient. After all this time, I am still putting my talent to good use, selecting only merchandise that I myself would buy or give to my family and friends.

Mon.- Sun. 10.00a - 10.00p

62-540 Kamehameha Hwy
Haleiwa, HI 96712
☎ 637-4737

Map1 / A2 73

THE LOMI SHOP

HAWAIIAN-STYLE THERAPEUTIC MASSAGE & PRODUCTS

Aloha mai! Experience the aloha touch of lomilomi, a Hawaiian healing art used to perpetuate health and wellness throughout Polynesia. Local practitioners have been called on a mission to educate, demonstrate and enhance the health of individuals and families. The Lomi Shop, famous for their foot massage, is an 'ohana (family) health center that offers full-body and seated chair massage. Polynesian Natural Health Products™ such as Tamanu oil from Tahiti, Noni, and other la'au lapa'au (medicinal herbs) are available. Explore and rediscover...

Voyaging through health & wellness

Aunty Malia Craver, Ka'uhane Lee, Moe Keale, Sandy Akana, Jarryd, Keola, Ku'ulei & Kepano From our 'ohana to yours... E O MAI!

Mon.- Sat.   10.00a - 9.00p
Sunday   10.00a - 5.00p

Windward Mall
Kane'ohe, HI 96744
☎ 234-5664
www.lomi.com

HAWAII MARTIAL ARTS SUPPLY

MARTIAL ARTS EQUIPMENT & ACCESSORIES

SOUTHSHORE OAHU

For 25 years, we have provided personalized service, quality products, and knowledge of all styles of martial arts. We have complete lines of martial arts supplies, from weapons, training equipment, and uniforms to breakthrough technology in magnetics.

Striving for physical, mental & spiritual balance thru martial arts

Walter & Ramona (father & daughter) President Walter Tang, C.P.A., has practiced tai chi for many years and has been affiliated with many community organizations. Ramona, youngest of seven children, has been the manager of Hawaii Martial Arts Supply, Inc., for the past 20 years and is the mother of a ten-year-old aikido student. She is also the owner of Good Fortune Basket Co., which specializes in homebaked goods and gift baskets.

Mon.- Fri.   8.30a - 4.00p
Saturday   8.30a - 3.00p

1041 Maunakea
Honolulu, HI 96817
☎ 536-5402

Map4 / C4 **75**

POWDER EDGE

OUTDOOR GEAR FOR PEOPLE WHO LIKE TO PLAY

We stock quality, functional
clothing and gear for people
who enjoy outdoor activities.
Whether it's rock climbing,
hiking, backpacking, surfing,
paddling, snowboarding, or
skiing, our employees (active
people who use our products
and wear our clothing) can
outfit you.

L M

*Quality &
functional
gear from
sea to ski!*

Mon.- Sat. 10.00a - 9.00p
Sunday   10.00a - 6.00p

1142 Auahi St (Ward Village Shops)
Honolulu, HI 96814
☎ 593-2267

John Nakajima (V.P.)
When John Nakajima established
Powder Edge in 1995, he found he
wasn't alone in discovering that
riding snow was just as much fun as
riding waves! He and Toru Otani (the
president) expanded the outdoor
concept to include a wide range of
quality gear and accessories.
People with active lifestyles have
discovered that Powder Edge is
THE place for their clothing and
accessories needs.

PRINCESS KAIULANI FASHIONS

& RIGGERS HAWAII, FINE ISLAND APPAREL

At our factory boutique you'll find casual resort wear, contemporary Hawaiian, formal, bridal attire, and Riggers Hawaii top-quality aloha shirts and sportswear... all priced at least 30% below regular retail! Relax in the "living room" setting while our friendly staff helps you find just what you need.

The spirit of Aloha

The Andersen Family

This family business, founded in 1959, is led by Jack and Joan Andersen. Jack, president; Joan, award-winning designer; Jon, owner of Riggers Hawaii; Judi, Miss USA 1978 & sales assoc.; Jay, artist for specialty apparel and home accents; and Jill, sales/production manager. Jill feels that "Although our styles are Hawaiian in theory, they are truly universal in nature."

Mon.- Sat.   9.00a - 5.00p
Sunday   10.00a - 3.00p

1220-1222 Kaumualii St.
Honolulu, HI 96817
☎ 847-4806
www.pkaiulanifashions.com

Map4 / C2 77

AMAZONIA FOREST

ENVIRONMENTALLY CONSCIOUS CLOTHING, ACCESSORIES & BEACHWEAR

Amazonia Forest was created to celebrate Mother Nature and the Earth on which we live. Colorful Brazilian and other South American and custom-designed beachwear, sportswear, leather goods, and accessories are features of our store, whose purpose is to make people feel comfortable, happy, and at one with the planet.

Keep the world green

Mon.- Sun. 10.00a - 6.00p

56-901 Kamehameha Hwy
Kahuku, HI 96712-0314
☎ 293-5053 Fax 293-9337
email. amazfores@aol.com

Cesar & Katia Oliveira (owner)
Cesar and Katia (currently expecting a new Oliveira!) opened Amazonia Forest's doors in 1992. "We feel that our store reflects the look, feel, and philosophy we believe in." Both are athletes and lovers of the outdoors, and their overriding goal is to create a greater awareness of the importance of preserving the environment.

HOME OF THE BRAVE

MEMORABILIA

We have World War II, Pan American Airways, and Hollywood memorabilia, as well as Hawaii surf gear, all under one roof. Shop for military flight jackets, hats, T-shirts, and one-of-a-kind souvenirs—and for handcrafted koa wood surfboards, skateboards, snowboards, canoe paddles, accessories, and surf wear. Taste delicious Kemoo Farms Happy Cakes while sipping on our own special coffee blends.

Glen Tomlinson (owner)
The shop reflects the lifelong interests of Glen, his wife Janet, and their three kids. Glen's travels (his parents worked for Pan American Airlines for 40 years) and knowledge of world history inspired his interactive tours of Oahu's military bases—"Home of the Brave Hawaii Military Base Tour and Top Gun Tours." His love of water sports and of the beauty and spirit of old Hawaii inspired Koa Surf Classics.

From generation to generation, the legacy lives on

Mon.- Fri. 9.00a - 3.00p
Sat.- Sun. By Appointment

909 Waimanu Street
Honolulu, HI, 96814
☎ 593-0747 & 396-8112

Map4 / D5 **79**

TROPICAL CLAY

HANDCRAFTED POTTERY

We've got banana leaf or anthurium flower plates and dinnerware to match your favorite tropical fish. Serve local style cuisine at home with our sashimi platters, chopstick holders, or saimin bowls with built-in chopstick rests. Plus, practical things (that you can't believe someone finally thought of) like bowls right-sized to hold exactly one can of your favorite soup. And, it's all microwaveable! Handpainted lamps and shades, clocks and even the bathroom sink are available in our designs or yours -- family crest, logo, or the fruit of your creative juices.

Our zany & talented artists specialize in fun, useable ceramics

Mario, Steve & Joel
Where does our inspiration come from? We just do what comes naturally in Hawaii—surf, fish, swim, dive, eat great food, and enjoy life with our family and friends. The things that make Hawaii special come through in our work.

Mon.- Sat.   10.00a - 9.00p
Sunday   10.00a - 5.00p

Ward Centre
Honolulu, Hawaii, 96814
☎ 597-1811

CHILD'S PLAY

EDUCATIONAL TOY STORE

Child'sPlay offers classic toys that stimulate creativity and develop essential motor skills and coordination. Even the toys that are "just for fun" establish a foundation for learning. Our staff, experienced in early childhood education, can assist you in selecting just the right toys for your special child.

Educational resource store for parents & teachers

Judy Eguchi (owner)
As a parent of two preshool children in the 1980's, I wanted more educationally oriented toys for them. Feeling a need for a store in metro Honolulu, I started Child'sPlay with the desire to bring good learning materials and classic playthings to parents and teachers. Over the past fifteen years, this concept has grown in popularity nationally, and I have a sense of pride and joy in having developed and nurtured the idea in Child'sPlay.

🌐
Mon.- Sat.   10.00a - 9.00p
Sunday   10.00a - 5.00p

Ward Warehouse
Honolulu, HI 96814
☎ 593-8863

Map4 / D5 (W1) **81**

KAMEHAMEHA
GARMENT CO.

VINTAGE HAWAIIAN APPAREL

The tropical design and furnishings are an inviting backdrop for our aloha shirts, dresses, men's and women's boardshorts, and vintage T-shirt line. We also personally select (from Bali and Lombok islands in Indonesia), imported jewelry, handbags, hats, and knicknacks, along with exclusive print sarongs. You can even order a custom-made longboard featuring inlays of the company's fabrics! Sample surfboards hang from the ceiling.

Hawaii's original aloha shirt manufacturer

Bobbi, Tammy & Josh (staff)
Founded in 1936 by Mr. Herb Briner, The Kamehameha Garment Co. was the first company in the Hawaiian Islands to manufacture and wholesale ready-to-wear garments. Today, under the leadership of Brad Walker, the Kamehameha Garment Company continues to make the shirts and sell them worldwide, along with an expanded line of sportswear for both men and women.

Mon.- Sat. 10.00a - 9.00p
Sunday   10.00a - 5.00p

Ward Centre
Honolulu, HI 96814
☎ 597-1503

DOONEY & BOURKE

HIGH-QUALITY LEATHER ITEMS

G H

Dooney & Bourke's Hawaii boutique is one of only three in America and features exclusive items only available at our boutiques. The famous "All-Weather Leather" collection includes handbags crafted in a waterproof cowhide that offers easy care—cleaning requires only a mild soap! Lightweight canvas cloth and naked leather are used in Dooney & Bourke's latest line, the "Cabriolet" collection. Cabriolet cloth is the same material used for convertible tops on such fine European cars as Mercedes Benz, BMW, and Porsche. Come see our stylish designs crafted in dependable, wearable, and durable leather.

*America's
favorite leather
brand!*

Mari & Henry (staff)
Dooney & Bourke is America's favorite leather brand. Uniquely American, all Dooney & Bourke products are handmade in the U.S.A.

🌐
Mon.- Sun. 9.00a - 11.00p

2335 Kalakaua Ave.
Honolulu, Hawaii 96815
☎ 922-0055

Map2 / B1 (RH) 83

BAIK DESIGNS

FURNITURE & INTERIOR ACCESSORIES

SOUTHSHORE · OAHU ·

G H

An antique bronze gamelan jostles for space with colorful batiks, primitive woodcarvings, and an elegant Eurasian wedding bed in the Iwilei showroom of Baik Designs. Its heirloom and eclectic furniture and interior accents have added a new twist to the tropical ambiance sought by everyone from Hollywood set designers to Islanders who want their surroundings to reflect an Island-style warmth. Interior designers and browsers alike can find museum-quality textiles, stunning statues, and stylish silver jewelry in this store that is big on one-of-a-kind treasures and personalized customer service.

Unique home furnishings

Mon.- Sat. 10.00a - 5.00p

560 N. Nimitz Hwy #108B
Honolulu, HI 96817
☎ 524-2290

Linda & Ed (owners)
Baik—Indonesian for "really good!"—is the culmination of a two-decade love affair of the owners with the islands of the former Dutch Indies. They personally travel to Indonesia and work with the country's top collectors, designers, and craftsmen to bring teak antiques and exotic coconut wood and elephant bamboo furniture to Hawaii.

Kauila Maxwell Co.

At Kauila Maxwell Company, everything is made in Hawaii. The industry leader in Hawaiian-made arts and apparel, we have, in addition, the finest collection of wooden bowls and rare Niʻihau shells on Oʻahu. Our signature apparel, home furnishings and accessories are designed around Hawaiian cultural elements, and we are proud of our attention to detail and to our customers.

*Honoring
Hawaiian
traditions*

Susan (owner), Keola, Lei, Ipo & Lin
As a part of the Hawaiian community, I am thrilled to be able to share my deep aloha for our culture. Whatever I do, whatever I design, I am always mindful and respectful of that culture.

Mon.- Sat. 10.00a - 9.00p
Sunday   10.00a - 5.00p

Windward Mall
Kaneohe, HI 96744
☎ 235-8383

Map3 / A2 (WM) 85

ROOTS & RELICS

NEW, USED, CLASSIC CLUBS & ACCESSORIES

Looking for that magic golf club to help your game, or that finely crafted classic club that brings back memories of years gone by? You'll find it at Roots & Relics, where avid golfers gather to peruse the hundreds of high-quality, reasonably priced putters, wedges, irons, and woods— from vintage hickory-shafted clubs to current high-tech equipment.

Golf clubs for beginners, pros & collectors

Tiffany

Owner Keith Tanaka is a Honolulu attorney whose hobby of collecting golf clubs and golf memorabilia soon became his profession. His collection, accumulated from across the country, now provides a "candy store" for golfers who are hunting for that perfect golf club.

Mon.- Fri.   10.30a - 5.00p
Saturday   12.00p - 3.00p

333 Queen Street
(corner of Queen & Richards St.)
Honolulu, HI 96813
☎ 538-3311

Na Lima Mili Hulu No'Eau

FEATHER LEI CLASSES AND SUPPLIES

We teach the art of feather lei making in both the traditional and the contemporary style. We also sell supplies for all your feather lei needs, including measures, clippers, third hands, and other tools and materials. Also available are student-made leis and special orders made by Aunty Mary Lou or Paulette.

* To continue to promote the fine art of feather lei making *

Aunty Mary Lou Kekuewa (owner)
Aunty Mary Lou Kekuewa was a student of Leilani Fernandez and began teaching in 1970 with the Queen Emma Hawaiian Civic Club. She is a life member of the Ahahui Kaahumanu Society & the National Society of Arts and Letters, and a member of the Hale O Na Alii. Aunty Mary Lou is a graduate of St. Andrew's Priory and taught feather lei making at the Bishop Museum for 25 years. She is the author of two books.

Mon.- Fri.   9.00a - 9.00p
Saturday   9.00a - 5.00p

762 Kapahulu Avenue
Honolulu, HI 96816
☎ 732-0865 Fax 737-3255

Map2 / B2 **87**

THE ORIGINAL RED DIRT SHIRT STORE

RETAIL SPORTSWEAR

For a special gift or a unique addition to your own wardrobe, check out the "good luck" gear at the Original Red Dirt Shirt Store. Our all-natural dye is made with pure Hawaiian Red Dirt, blessed according to Hawaiian tradition, and believed to bring good luck to the wearer. Choose from many 100% cotton, highest-quality T-shirt styles and hundreds of beautiful designs created by local artists. We also carry Red Dirt accessories, such as caps, socks, earrings, pendants, scrunchies, and, yes, Red Dirt Soap!

Winner of Hawaii's prestigious "Unique Fashion Award"

Mon.- Sat.   9.00a - 9.00p
Sunday   9.00a - 6.00p

Aloha Tower Marketplace
Honolulu, HI 96816
☎ 524-0778

A Few Of Our Red Dirt Crew
The tradewinds kept blowing Hawaii's powdery Red Dirt all over his beautifully silk screened T-shirts, so "Bob" Hedin, our President, decided to work WITH Mother Nature instead of against her. Using the dirt's powerful staining properties to formulate an all-natural dye, the Original Red Dirt Shirt line debuted with 5 designs in Nov. '93 and the shirts were an instant hit! Hundreds of designs later, Original Red Dirt Shirts are now worn by happy customers worldwide.

XTREME PAINTBALL SUPPLY

W H O L E S A L E ,   R E T A I L   &   R E P A I R S

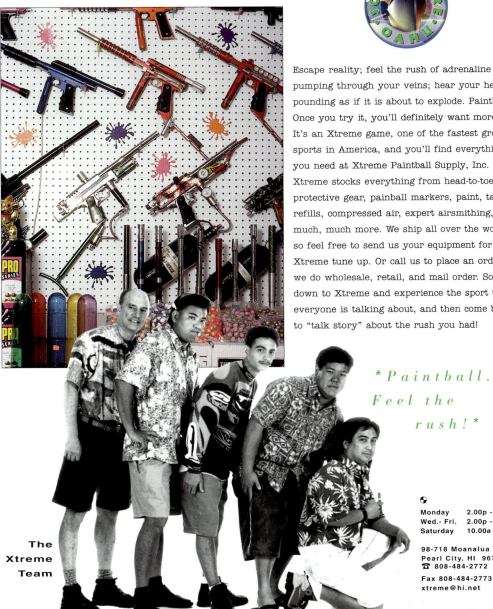

Escape reality; feel the rush of adrenaline pumping through your veins; hear your heart pounding as if it is about to explode. Paintball— Once you try it, you'll definitely want more. It's an Xtreme game, one of the fastest growing sports in America, and you'll find everything you need at Xtreme Paintball Supply, Inc. Xtreme stocks everything from head-to-toe: protective gear, painball markers, paint, tank refills, compressed air, expert airsmithing, and much, much more. We ship all over the world, so feel free to send us your equipment for an Xtreme tune up. Or call us to place an order, we do wholesale, retail, and mail order. So come down to Xtreme and experience the sport that everyone is talking about, and then come back to "talk story" about the rush you had!

*Paintball.
Feel the
rush!*

**The
Xtreme
Team**

Monday	2.00p - 9.00p
Wed.- Fri.	2.00p - 10.00p
Saturday	10.00a - 10.00p

98-718 Moanalua Road
Pearl City, HI 96782
☎ 808-484-2772

Fax 808-484-2773
xtreme@hi.net

Map4 / Inset **89**

PROSPERITY CORNER

METAPHYSICAL

At Prosperity Corner, magnificent magic is occurring all the time. All of our staff are professional psychics (most practice some form of magic as well). Whether you're looking for tarot, astrology, runes, numerology, palmistry, tea leaf readings, or reiki, we have a psychic for you. If you want to increase your personal power, ask about our classes. We also have one of the largest tarot card collections in Hawaii, as well as books, essential oils, crystals, and one-of-a-kind jewelry, and offer hand-painted body art, mehndi, and exotic piercings.

There's a new spirit in Kaimuki

D.J. Colbert And Staff

Mon.- Sat.   10.00a - 7.00p
Sunday   12.00p - 6.00p

3619 Waialae Avenue
Honolulu, HI 96816
☎ 732-8870

ARTS HAWAII, INC.

CUSTOM GLASS ETCHERS

LM

Each item is hand drawn, cut, and etched at our workshop to create a unique treasure to cherish or to give with pride and love.

A Hawaii
tradition
since 1946

Gary Oda (owner)
Started in 1946 by my father, Frank Y. Oda, as Hale Pua, Arts Hawaii has served the gift and design needs of a large local, national, and international clientele, including several royal clients. I returned to take over the family business in 1972 after several years of art training in Europe. From my parents I have learned that the customer is always to be treated with kindness and as a friend.

Mon.- Fri.   9.30a - 5.00p
Saturday   10.00a - 2.00p

514 Piikoi Street
Honolulu, HI 96814
☎ 591-2544

Map4 / D6 **91**

FOLLOWING SEA

A SHOP & GALLERY

Stepping into Following Sea is like stepping into another world. To paraphrase Steinbeck, a poem, a quality of light, a feeling, a tone. A gathering of work from the hands of this country's foremost craft artists is displayed in a serene and soothing space where the works speak for themselves. Whether shopping for yourself or looking for the perfect gift, you are sure to find treasures among the unique bowls, boxes, jewelry, pottery, clothing, and other handcrafted items. We also have some of the most beautiful books you will find anywhere.

Makana aloha:
*"gift of friendship or love"**

🌐
Mon.- Sat.   10.00a - 9.00p
Sunday   10.00a - 5.00p

Kahala Mall
Honolulu, HI 96816
☎ 734-4425

Sheila Kawakami (mgr.)
Our competent staff is thoroughly
familiar with the artists and
artistic processes represented at
Following Sea.

FLAGS FLYING

ALL THINGS FLAGS

Flags Flying is a unique store where the flags of the world are our business. In addition to the largest selection of decorator flags and windsocks, we have flag fashions and accessories: T-shirts, sweatshirts, shorts, jackets, caps, mugs, lapel pins, patches, decals, watches, and flag poles. We are also Hawaii's premier producer of custom flags and banners.

Flag provider to the Pacific—colors of the world

Hy & Nornie Rosenstein (owners)
Five years in business has made Flags Flying the outstanding flag merchandiser in the Pacific, with a full range of products representing Hawaii, the other U.S. states and territories, and foreign countries.

Mon.- Sat.   9.00a - 9.00p
Sunday   9.00a - 6.00p

Aloha Tower Marketplace
Honolulu, HI 96813
☎ 537-1300

Map4 / D4 (AT) **93**

CHOCOLATES FOR BREAKFAST LIFESTYLES

SPECIALTY WOMEN'S SHOP

GH

Chocolates For Breakfast (CFB) Lifestyles was created to fulfill the every need of the woman of the new millennium. Inviting interior design, timeless fashions and accessories, fashion forward designer collections and fine European lingerie. You will fall in love with their exclusive "Arcona" line of all-natural body and skin care, aromatherapies, and unique lifestyle gifts. CFB Lifestyles has become the #1 fashion destination for an extensive list of international clientele, island and mainstream celebrities. Their experienced staff will coordinate and accessorize a wardrobe uniquely your own and offer the "most wanted" lifestyle gifts. As you know, the gift one gives is an extension of the gift giver's unique style.

Mon.- Sat.   10.00a - 9.00p
Sunday   10.00a - 5.00p

Ward Warehouse
Honolulu, HI 96814
☎ 808-596-0667

Fax 808-593-0069

Create memories to cherish for a lifetime

Audrey Fu (owner)
For over three decades, owner Audrey Fu has been Hawaii's leading fashion authority —living and exemplifying fashion's many trends and transformations. Audrey hosted a weekly fashion segment on the morning news, and she has judged numerous beauty pageants. Chocolates For Breakfast has also dressed many Hawaii women who have gone on to become successful actresses, Miss America, and most recently, Miss Universe 1997!

THE CONTEMPORARY MUSEUM SHOP

AT THE CONTEMPORARY MUSEUM

"We don't have the cute little bags with handles, but visitors claim we have the best selection of handcrafted and contemporary one-of-a-kind items they've ever seen." It's true. Art jewelry, books, and accessories are not the same ol', same ol' you find in other shops. Arresting images, riotous color, and tactile experiences. That's what you'll find at the Contemporary Museum Shop.

*Where art
is alive
and well...*

**Barbara Rau (shop mgr.) &
Betsy Robertson (asst. mgr.)**

Tue.- Sat.   10.00a - 4.00p
Sunday   12.00p - 4.00p

2411 Makiki Heights Dr.
Honolulu, HI 96822
☎ 808-523-3477

Map4 / B6 **95**

SILVERMOON EMPORIUM

WOMEN'S CLOTHING BOUTIQUE

Silvermoon provides one of the most memorable shopping experiences in the islands. The store was beautifully designed by co-owner Wayne Holu; it inspires a sense of elegance and nostalgia. Whether you're shopping for yourself or a loved one, you will find beautiful displays, quality merchandise, and personal, individualized service and advice.

Everything unique under one roof

Mon.- Sun. 10.00a - 6.00p

66250 Kam Hwy #G170
Haleiwa, HI 96712
☎ 637-7710

Lucie Talbot-Holu (owner) at 6
As a young girl growing up in Montreal, Lucie never grew tired of dress-up, makeovers, and Barbie dolls. She entered the real world of fashion by becoming a "personal shopper" for an elite group of executive women. Her duties included head-to-toe dressing for all occasions— TV appearances, cocktail parties, and power meetings. In 1989, she established Silvermoon Emporium, her idea of the "perfect store," with everything today's woman needs—gifts, unique clothing, accessories, even fragrances, lingerie, footwear, and home decorations.

HONOLULU PEN SHOP

FINE WRITING INSTRUMENTS/ACCESSORIES

Our shop is part showroom, part museum—a relaxing place to try out Hawaii's largest selection of new and vintage writing instruments, including Cartier, Montblanc, Waterman, Cross, Pelikan, Parker, Namiki, Montegrappa and others. Our goal is to match the individual to his or her perfect fountain pen, ball point, rollerball, or pencil.

* Where handwriting finds the personal touch *

Earl Shigemoto (owner)

A recognized authority on quality writing instruments, owner Earl Shigemoto has over 25 years' experience in fountain pen repair, sales and service. His own collection of rare fountain pens is one of the country's finest. Shigemoto personally assists every customer. "The only way to buy a pen is to try it. Like people themselves, every pen has its own personality. It has to be inked up and touched to paper to see how it suits the hand that holds it."

Mon.- Fri.   9.00a - 6.00p
Saturday   10.00a - 5.00p

1857 South King St. #100
Honolulu, HI 96826
☎ 808-946-8968

Map2 / A2 **97**

EUROPEAN VILLAGE

GOURMET FOOD AND DRINK

European Village/ La Sardine, an elegant store designed by the talented Sandi Quildon, offers a new definition of spiritual and earthly desires. The delicacies we offer feed the soul as well as the body.

Harmony between the sense of the eye & palate

Mon.- Sun. 9.30a - 10.30p

2201 Kalakaua Ave.
3rd Flr. Hibiscus Court
Honolulu, HI 96815
☎ 923-1777

Hana (owner)

Hana Messaouda Kheddaoui was born in the Sahara desert to a family who formed many ties with France. Hana studied at the Sorbonne and the Louvre, where her interests in the culinary field developed. Her frequent travels in the Mediterranean world enhanced her knowledge of fine cuisine. Encouraged by friends (chefs, oenologues, and epicureans), she came to Hawaii, where she had a vision that Waikiki's unique sophistication made it the ideal place to continue her gourmet life.

SWING SONG

HAMMOCKS, WIND CHIMES & SPECIALTY GIFTS

Work-of-art hammocks and wind chimes from around the world enhance the indoor and outdoor décor of any home—while they lower blood pressure and increase relaxation! We have traditional and non-traditional hammocks in a wide array of fabrics, sizes, and styles, plus Hawaii's largest array of wind chimes, from mini to maxi—with prices to suit every pocketbook. We accept all major credit cards and ships worldwide.

It just isn't paradise without hammocks & wind chimes!

Victor & Tamara (owners)
What happens when a guy who works at a hammock shop meets a gal who works at a wind chime shop? Magic, both professional and personal. For Victor Miceli and the former Tamara Weinstein it meant forming a lifelong partnership and opening Hawaii's premier hammock, wind chime, and specialty gift shop.

Mon.- Sat.   9.00a - 9.00p
Sunday   9.00a - 6.00p

Aloha Tower Marketplace #177
Honolulu, HI 96813
☎ 536-8825 Fax 524-8953

Map4 / D4 (AT) **99**

FLOREXOTICA HAWAII

SILK FOLIAGE & CHRISTMAS PRODUCTS

We make UN-real plants that fool the eye—maybe even Mother Nature! Our plants and flowers look like the real thing, but don't need watering, fertilizing, or pruning. Buy for yourself or send a ho'okupu (gift). We safely ship around the world via insured priority mail. We love seeing the smiles on our customers' faces when we can help them find that perfect something. Please visit our web site at www.florexotica.com for more info. Just opened: our new store 1 mile outside of Waikiki at 1253 South Beretania St. (808) 593-7903.

There is only one way to do a job— WELL!

U'ilani Stender & cousins Ke'aulumoku & 'Aipohaku Durant

--the future of Hawaii!!!!

Established in 1980, Florexotica Hawaii is a Hawaiian company run by Hawaiians—Lei-Ann Stender-Durant and her brother, Patrick Stender. We are dedicated to providing high-quality, economical products to people who love exotic plants but don't have time to cultivate and care for them.

Mon.- Fri.   8.00a - 4.30p

500 Ala Kawa St. #210
Honolulu, HI 96817
☎ 842-5166

have we missed

anybody?

"Mahalo iā 'oukou

pākahi a pau"

Acknowlegments

(Thanks to each and everyone)

kula abiva • greg barbour • ruth ann becker • jan berman • mark bernstein • richard bluefarb • scott creel • heidi di'eugenio • roger dubin • paulina evans • extra-strength tylenol • james faumuina • monica fulton • mufi hannemann • laurie hara • osamu hayakawa • jimi hendrix • jane hopkins • becky huffman • paul klink • francis lam • jada london • scott mccormack • maile meyer • jon miho • tom moffatt • david nada • stephanie nagata • hiromi nagata • oahu visitors bureau • valery o'brien • sandy haunani oguma • ruthann quitiquit • retail merchants of hawaii • noelani schilling-wheeler • reve shapard • barbara sheehan • mike and hal @snapshot • state of hawaii dbed & t • keith stevenson • dexter suzuki • valerie sylvester • patrick, ron, david, wayne and tracey@valenti brothers • charlian wright • our moms & dads • & anyone we missed was only a momentary lapse, not forgotten!

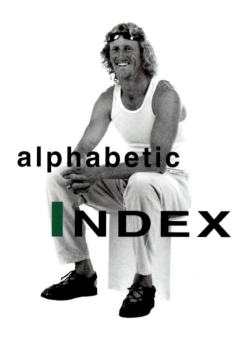

alphabetic
INDEX

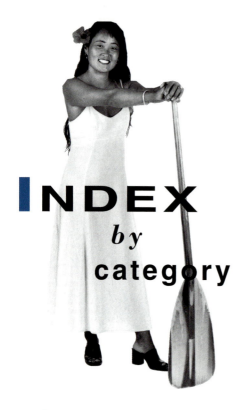

INDEX
by
category

drink

Oahu Home Brew: *beer & wine-making supplies* 57
Vin Glace: *fine canadian icewine* 55
Vintage Wine Cellar: *fine wines, spirits & accessories* 14

kitchen

The Compleat Kitchen: *kitchen specialty shop* 12
The Kitchen & Spice Co.: *gourmet spices, foods & kitchen accessories* 51

health & wellness

Kaimuki Health Market: *healthy foods & supplements* 8
The Lomi Shop: *hawaiian style therapeutic massage and health products* 74
Prosperity Corner: *metaphysical* 90

sports/hobby

808 Skate: *skateboards & accessories* 17
Blue Hawaii Surf: *surfboards & accessories* 33
Eki Cyclery: *bicycles & accessories* 2
Hana Pa'a Hawaii: *fishing supplies* 7
Hawaii Martial Arts Supply: *martial arts equipment & accessories* 75
Naish Hawaii Ltd: *windsurfing wholesale, rental, sales, repair & lessons* 38
Other Realms: *comics & games* 45
The Pacific Hobbyist: *plastic model shop* 65
Powder Edge: *outdoor gear* 76
Roots & Relics: *golf: new, used, classic clubs & accessories* 86
Russ•K Makaha: *longboard surf shop* 63
Xtreme Paintball: *wholesale, retail & repairs* 89

jewelry

Black Pearl Gallery: *jewelry as rare & exotic as you are* 21
Hawaiian Heirloom Jewelry Factory & Museum: *by philip rickard* 35
Opal Fields: *fine jewelry & gems* 28

hawaiiana

Kauila Maxwell Co.: *hawaiian-made arts, gifts, apparel* 85
Na Lima Mili Hulu No'eau: *feather-lei classes & supplies* 87
Native Books & Beautiful Things: *hawaiian artists' cooperative* 36
Quilts Hawaii: *quality comforters, plus...* 52

imports/gifts

Outrigger Trading Co.: *fine gifts & collectibles* 73
Siam Imports: *treasures from thailand* 56
Artlines: *a grand bazaar* 11

museum shops

Bishop Museum: *museum gift shops* 69
Contemporary Museum: *museum art/gifts* 95

handicrafts/art

Arts Hawaii, Inc.: *custom glass etchers* 91
Island Treasures: *art gallery* 22
Jeff Chang Pottery: *fine crafts gallery* 47
Oceans In Glass: *art from the depths of soul & sea* 70

galleries/gifts

Following Sea: *a shop & gallery* 92
Kim Taylor Reece Gallery: *fine art photography* 43
Lance Fairly Gallery: *fine art & gifts* 6
Nohea Gallery: *island art & fine crafts* 1

specialty

The Bead Gallery: *beads, jewelry, workshops* 16
Bookends: *a special book store* 30
Calico General Store: *country-style store* 27
Fire It Up!: *ceramics painting studio* 32
Flags Flying: *all things flags* 93
Florexotica: *silk foliage & christmas products* 100
Flyin' Hawaiian balloons: *full service balloons* 50
Global Village Market: *hemp•aromatherapy•jewelry•apparel•gifts* 5
Hawaiian Rent All: *general store of rentals* 10
Home Of The Brave: *memorabilia* 79
Honolulu Pen Shop: *fine writing instruments & accessories* 97
Island Guitars: *new/used/vintage instruments* 71
Koolau Farmers: *retail garden shop* 24
Marsha Nadalin Salon & Spa: *full-service salon & day spa* 39
McClain Auctions: *auctions, antiques & more* 60
Needlepoint, Etc.: *supplies & instruction* 34
SnapShot: *photo equipment & services* 9
The Ukulele House: *where ukuleles live* 40

OAHU

WINDWARD · OAHU

DIAMONDHEAD · OAHU

SOUTHSHORE · OAHU

NORTHSHORE · OAHU

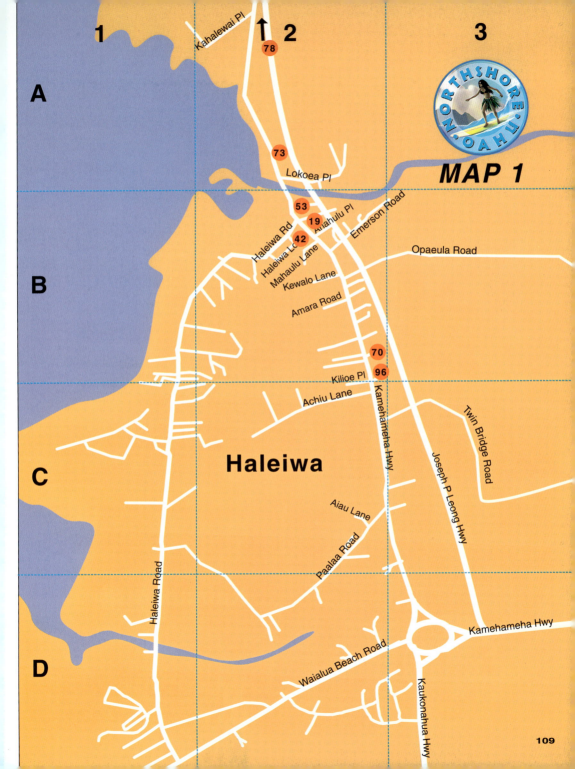

1 **2** **3**

Kahalewai Pl

78

A

NORTHSHORE, O'AHU

MAP 1

73

Lokoea Pl

Emerson Road

53

Anahulu Pl

19

Opaeula Road

Haleiwa Rd

42

Haleiwa Lo

Mahaulu Lane

Kewalo Lane

B

Amara Road

70

96

Kilioe Pl

Achiu Lane

Kamehameha Hwy

Twin Bridge Road

Joseph P Leong Hwy

C

Haleiwa

Aiau Lane

Haleiwa Road

Paalaa Road

Kamehameha Hwy

D

Waialua Beach Road

Kaukonahua Hwy

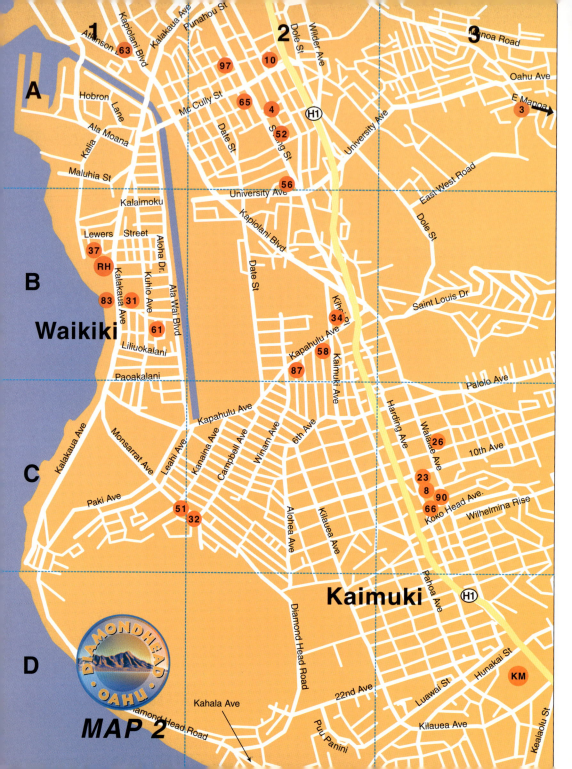

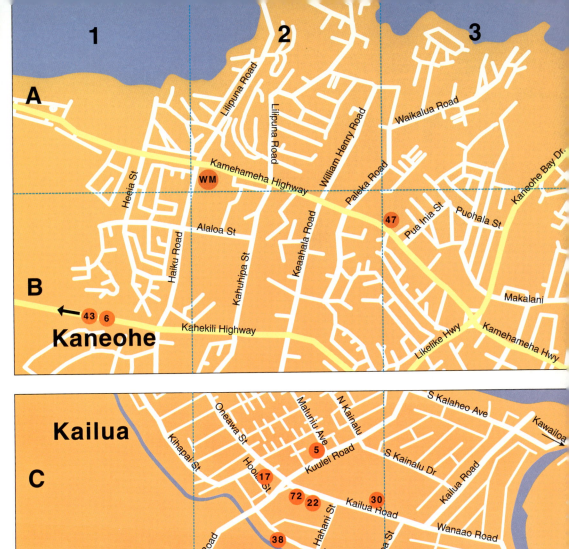

1 **2** **3**

A

Liilipuna Road

Liilipuna Road

William Henry Road

Waikalua Road

Kaneohe Bay Dr.

Heeia St

Kamehameha Highway

WM

Alaloa St

Paleka Road

47

Pua Inia St

Puohala St

Kahuhipa St

Keaahala Road

Haiku Road

Makalani

B

43 **6**

Kaneohe

Kahekili Highway

Likelike Hwy

Kamehameha Hwy

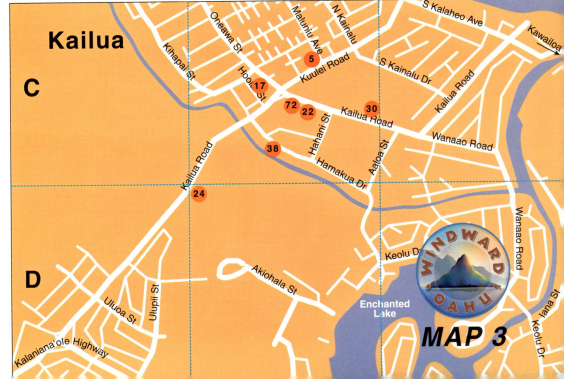

Kailua

Oneawa St

Maluniu Ave

N Kainalu

S Kalaheo Ave

Kawailoa

Kihapai St

5

Kuulei Road

S Kainalu Dr

Kailua Road

C

Hoolai St

17

72 **22**

30

Kailua Road

Wanaao Road

Hahani St

Aaloa St

38

Hamakua Dr

Kailua Road

24

Keolu Dr

Wanaao Road

D

Ulupii St

Akiohala St

Uluoa St

Kalaniana'ole Highway

Enchanted Lake

Keolu Dr

Iana St

WINDWARD OAHU

MAP 3

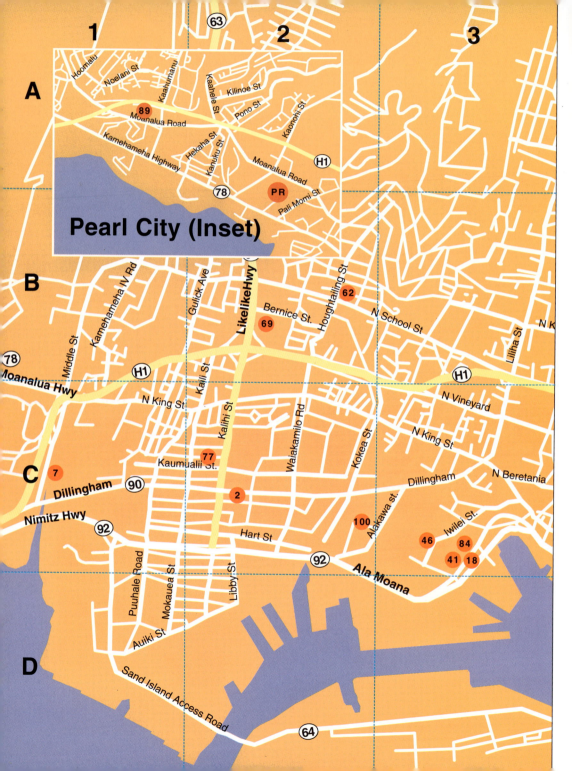

Pearl City (Inset)

1 **2** **3**

63

A

Hoomalu
Noelani St
Kaahumanu
Kaahele St
Kilinoe St
Pono St
Kaonohi St
89
Moanalua Road
Kamehameha Highway
Hekaha St
Kanuku St
Moanalua Road
H1
78
P R
Pali Momi St

B

Kamehameha IV Rd
Gulick Ave
Likelike Hwy
Houghtailing St
62
Bernice St.
N School St
69
Liliha St
N K
Middle St
78
Moanalua Hwy
H1
Kalii St
N King St
Kalihi St
Waiakamilo Rd
Kokea St
N Vineyard
N King St
H1

C
7
Dillingham
90
Kaumualii St.
77
2
Dillingham
N Beretania
Nimitz Hwy
92
Hart St
100
Alakawa st.
46
Iwilei St.
84
41 **18**
92
Ala Moana
Puuhale Road
Mokauea St
Libby St

D

Auiki St
Sand Island Access Road
64

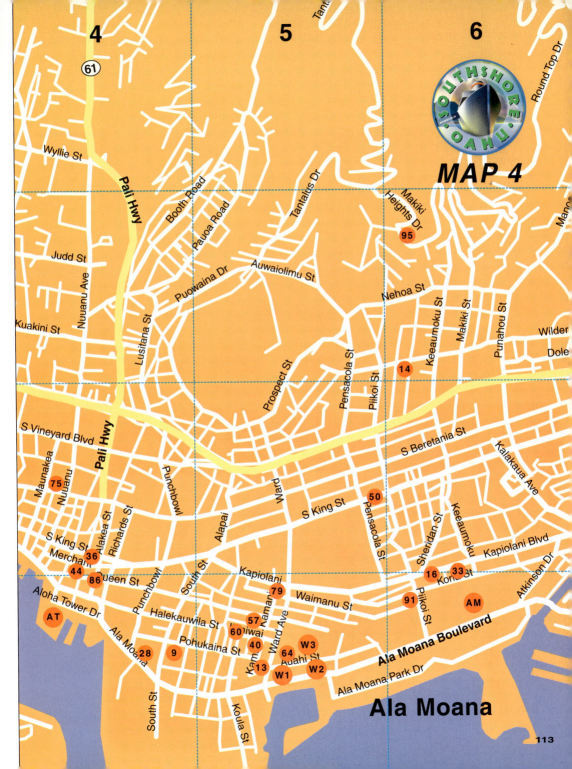

Team u.s.
(oʻahu)

(L to R)
Gary Hoffheimer	*store photographer "tex"*
Michael Poe	*art director "frenchie"*
Norma Spierings	*project manager "mom"*
Patrick Tozier	*sales "big daddy"*
Ian Gillespie	*sales & production "x-man"*
Chad Kahunahana	*sales "loco boy"*
Scott Tilsley	*studio manager "bear"*
Linny Morris	*store photographer "the hipster"*
Hugh O'Reilly	*glue "voodoo chile"*
Ian	*1st gofer "wolf"*
Sergio Goes	*portrait photographer "samba"*
(not shown) **Laura Lee**	*sales "surfer girl"*
(not shown) **Bob Franklin**	*cartographer/illustrator "tomorrow"*

(concept, design, production & coordination
by FXproductions)

Tel. 808-689-0020

Fax 808-689-0026

www.UltimateShoppers.com

91-025 Popoi Place, Honolulu, HI 96706

Notes